BELIZE
in Pictures

Tom Streissguth

Twenty-First Century Books

Contents

Twenty-First Century Books
A division of Lerner Publishing Group, Inc.
241 First Avenue North
Minneapolis, MN 55401 U.S.A.

Website address: www.lernerbooks.com

web enhanced @ www.vgsbooks.com

Library of Congress Cataloging-in-Publication Data

Streissguth, Thomas, 1958-
      Belize in pictures / by Tom Streissguth.
      p.   cm. — (Visual geography series)
      Includes bibliographical references and index.
      ISBN 978-1-57505-958-7 (lib. bdg. : alk. paper)
      1. Belize—Juvenile literature. I. Title.
F1443.2.S77 2010
972.82—dc22   2008038027

Manufactured in the United States of America
1 2 3 4 5 6 – BP – 15 14 13 12 11 10

INTRODUCTION

A small nation in Central America, Belize lies between two worlds: the Caribbean region and Central America. Belize was once the heartland of the Maya, an indigenous (native) American culture that dominated the region for more than a thousand years. Belize was later home to pirates, loggers, former slaves, and refugees of civil wars in Mexico and the United States. The modern Belizean nation is a patchwork of different cultures and languages.

In 1862 Belize became a British colony known as British Honduras. The area remained poor and isolated through the middle of the twentieth century. The colony saw little foreign investment. Economically, British Honduras relied on logging and agriculture. Little manufacturing or mining took place, few tourists came to the colony, and other service industries were small. In addition, settlement was sparse. Only a few large towns hugged the coastline. Inland, there were few roads and only one small railway.

After World War II (1939–1945), the people of British Honduras

demanded independence. After many years of debate and negotiations, Belize won full independence in 1981. Its government held open, peaceful elections. The country avoided the civil strife that affected many other nations in Central America.

In the meantime, tourism picked up. In fact, it brought an economic boom to the nation. In the twenty-first century, Belize welcomes more than one million visitors a year. They come to see the nation's historic Mayan ruins, beautiful landscape, and many kinds of wildlife. Many outsiders are moving to Belize permanently. Foreigners are buying property and building homes and resorts.

This new investment brings development and jobs. It also brings problems. Roads and other infrastructure (public works such as water systems) are in need of repair. New construction is affecting resources and threatens the natural environment. And some government leaders have faced charges of corruption regarding how they handle the invested money. Such charges affect the people's trust in their leaders.

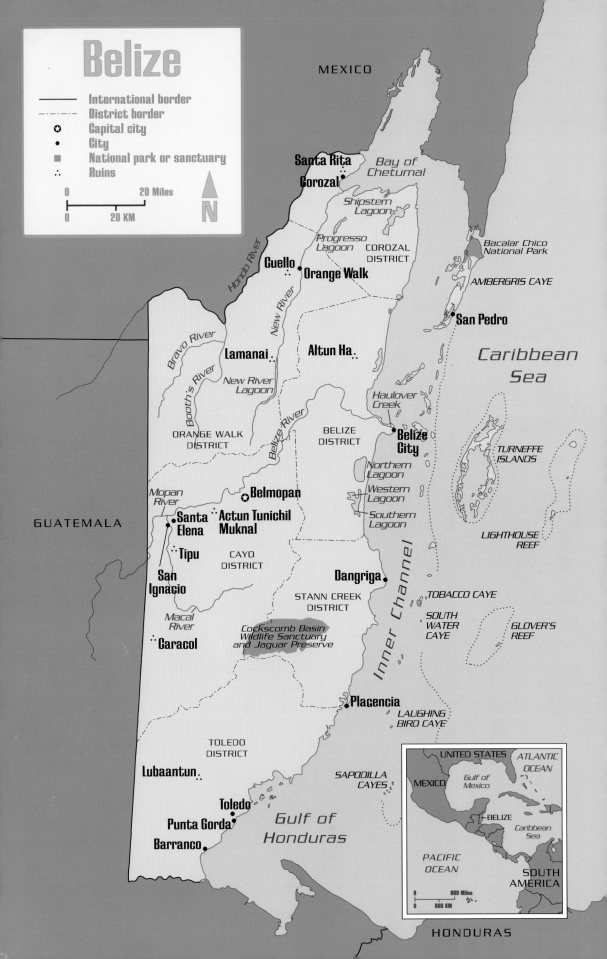

The balance between development and the environment is an important challenge facing modern Belize. To attract visitors, the country must protect its many natural wonders. But Belize needs and welcomes foreign investment. It allows many foreign companies to build resorts, hotels, residences, and port facilities.

From a long and complex history, Belize has developed a vital and diverse culture. As a former British colony, its culture is distinct from that of its Spanish-settled Central American neighbors. In addition, descendants of African slaves, known as the Garinagu, have their own artistic and musical styles. The Maya also carry on their cultural traditions and still speak the Mayan language in small villages of the south. At the same time, a new wave of settlement is coming from Mexico and Central America. These newcomers bring the Spanish language and their own ways of life. Belize also is home to a community of Mennonites. This religious community rejects many modern ways, yet Mennonites have built many of the nation's most productive farms.

Belize remains a country off the beaten track. It has limited road and air connections to the outside world. Relatively few jobs exist for skilled and college-educated citizens. Many Belizeans have emigrated, seeking better opportunities abroad. Nevertheless, Belize has avoided many of the conflicts and problems of developing countries. Despite its challenges, the strengths of this nation of 300,000 people give it bright prospects for the future.

THE LAND

Belize is a nation of Central America that lies along the western shores of the Caribbean Sea. To the north is Mexico. The Bay of Chetumal separates northern Belize from a long coastal peninsula belonging to the Mexican province of Quintana Roo. (A peninsula is a stretch of land bordered on three sides by water.) Guatemala borders Belize to the west. The Gulf of Honduras—part of the Caribbean Sea—forms Belize's southern border. Belize shares this wide, island-studded bay with two other Central American nations, Guatemala and Honduras.

With a land area of 8,867 square miles (22,965 square kilometers), Belize is slightly smaller than the U.S. state of Massachusetts. Belize stretches 174 miles (280 km) from its northernmost to its southernmost point. From east to west, Belize is only 68 miles (109 km) across. Belize is the second-smallest nation in Central America, after El Salvador. And it is the only nation in Central or North America without a shore on the Pacific Ocean.

Topography

Belize has four main geographic regions. From east to west, they are the Cayes and Barrier Reef, the Coastal Lowlands, the Central Plains, and the Western Highlands.

Off the coast of Belize, the waters of the Inner Channel separate the mainland from the Cayes and Barrier Reef. The cayes are small islands that form an archipelago (island chain). Near the cayes lies the barrier reef. Made up of underwater creatures called corals, this barrier reef extends 185 miles (298 km) from north to south. It is the world's second-largest coral reef, after the Great Barrier Reef in Australia.

Belize's cayes include, from north to south, Ambergris Caye, Tobacco Caye, South Water Caye, Laughing Bird Caye, and the Sapodilla Cayes. Farther offshore are the Turneffe Islands, Lighthouse Reef, and Glover's Reef. The cayes have sandy, infertile soil and thick stands of mangrove trees. Over the ages, the islets and reefs appear and disappear with the shifting of the seafloor.

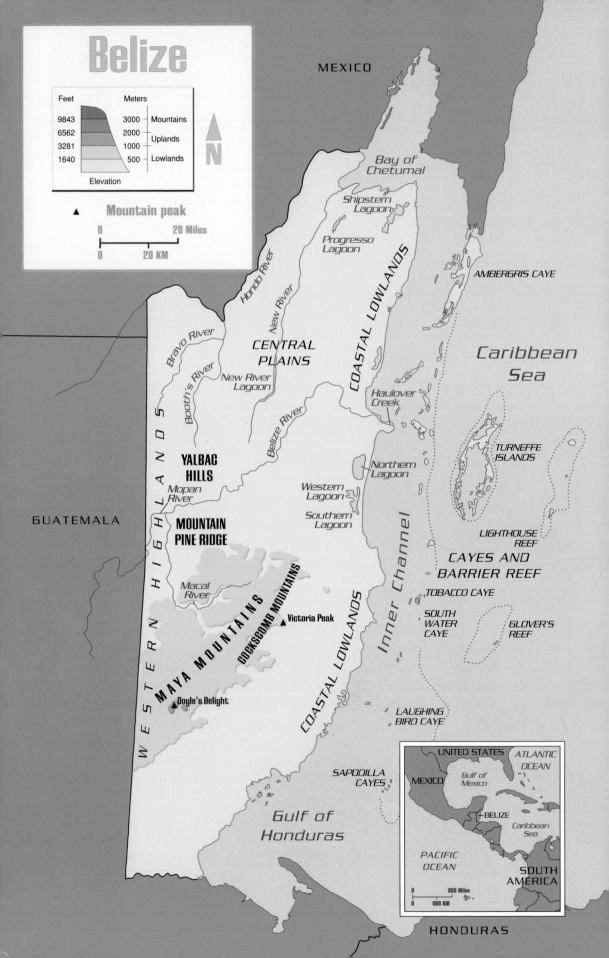

The Coastal Lowlands form a belt of land in eastern Belize, along the nation's coast. In this region, the average elevation is about 200 feet (61 meters) above sea level. Several thousand years ago, much of this low-lying plain was part of the seafloor. In modern times, a series of bays and lagoons line the coast.

Inland, these lowlands meet the Central Plains. Fertile soil covers this land, and Belizeans here raise bananas and sugarcane on plantations (large commercial farms). Farmers have cleared trees for crop fields and fruit orchards. Grasslands called savannas cover much of this central region. The land is relatively flat, with sparse vegetation and scattered stands of trees. Unpaved roads link small towns that lie along the waterways.

From the plains, the land gradually rises to become the Western Highlands. The Yalbac Hills run near the western border with Guatemala. Southwest of the city of Belmopan, the Mountain Pine Ridge rises to more than 3,000 feet (914 m). These foothills make up the northern edge of the Maya Mountains. The soil in the region is poor. For this reason, the Mountain Pine Ridge has always had very sparse settlement. Geologists believe the Mountain Pine Ridge is the oldest landform in Central America. Elevation rises further in the Maya Mountains, a region of granite hills and outcrops in south central Belize and eastern Guatemala. Few roads or settlements exist in the

Forests of tropical trees blanket Belize's Maya Mountains in the southern portion of the country.

region. The highest point in Belize, a peak known as Doyle's Delight, reaches 3,688 feet (1,124 m) within the Cockscomb Mountains. Fast-flowing rivers in these highlands cut short and narrow valleys through a tropical rain forest. Water erosion (wearing away) of rock and soil has carved underground caves and sinkholes. Heavy rainfall nourishes many varieties of orchids, ferns, and climbing vines.

◎ Rivers and Lakes

The Belize River is the country's main waterway. The Belize flows through central Belize before emptying into the sea at Belize City. Belizeans also know this waterway as the Old River. It served as a main transportation route for centuries. Beginning in the 1600s, loggers also used the river to float their timber downstream to the sea. A small branch of the river, Haulover Creek, flows through Belize City before reaching the Caribbean.

The northern plains of Belize contain several small rivers, including the Bravo River and Booth's River. The Hondo River forms the border with Mexico. The New River passes the ancient Mayan city of Lamanai and flows northeastward to its mouth on the Bay of Chetumal. This waterway served the Maya as a busy trade route. Its surrounding area has been a center of cultivation for many centuries. Sugarcane plantations and crop fields stretch away from the river in the surrounding lowlands.

The Macal and the Mopan rivers rise in the foothills of the Maya Mountains. These rivers form the headwaters (source) of the Belize River. Water levels in these rivers vary with the seasons. During rainy months, the rivers are wide and fast flowing. They branch into several streams and in places overflow into small lakes and pools. These rivers carry abundant fertile soil to the central plains. Crocodiles and turtles paddle in the shallows and sun themselves on the riverbanks.

In northern Belize, the New River widens into the New River Lagoon, the nation's largest body of freshwater. Other lagoons include Progresso and Shipstern in the north and the Northern, Western, and Southern lagoons southwest of Belize City.

WHAT'S A BELIZE?

The name of Belize may come from the Mayan word *belix*, which means "muddy water." This pretty well describes the Belize River, the country's main waterway. Otherwise, the name may come from the Spanish pronunciation of "Wallace." Peter Wallace is the name of a Scottish pirate who was the first European to settle in the territory in 1638.

Belmopan is less mysterious. *Bel* comes from the word Belize, and "Mopan" is the name of a Mayan people who lived in the region.

A family travels by canoe on the New River. The New River is the longest river contained entirely within Belize. Visitors may glimpse crocodiles and iguanas sunning themselves on the river's banks.

Climate

Belize lies within the tropics. Tropical countries are located near the equator between the Tropic of Cancer and the Tropic of Capricorn. The warm, humid climate varies little from season to season. A trade wind blows toward the equator, or the belt around the center of Earth. This wind blows across the country from the northeast, cooling the temperatures and bringing precipitation.

Belize has two main seasons. A rainy season runs through the summer and fall. A dry season begins in late winter. Weather also varies slightly with elevation and distance from the sea. In coastal areas, winds blow from the Caribbean Sea. They cool the tropical heat but also bring rain and humidity. Year-round temperatures in lowland areas range from a daytime high of 95°F (35°C) to a nightly low of 60°F (16°C). In Belize City, rainfall averages 65 inches (165 centimeters) a year. The coolest month is usually January, and the warmest is May.

The dry season is much shorter in southern Belize than in the north. A short and rainless period known as the little dry sometimes occurs in the middle of the summer. In the Maya Mountains and other highlands, temperatures are cooler and humidity is lower. Annual precipitation in the north and in mountainous areas reaches about 50 inches (127 cm). Rainfall is heavier in the south, averaging about 150 inches (381 cm) per year.

Hurricanes, which strike from late summer through the fall, have a major impact on Belize. These giant storms surge across the Caribbean from the east. As they draw warm, moist air from the sea, the storms

Waves crash against a seawall in the northern city of Corozal during Hurricane Dean, which struck the coast in 2007.

gain energy. Two major hurricanes in the mid-twentieth century devastated Belize City, the nation's former capital, with high winds and flooding. The threat of further damage convinced the authorities to move the national capital inland, to the new city of Belmopan.

Flora and Fauna

A sparsely populated country, Belize has a wealth of natural habitats. Although timber cutting has been an important activity for centuries, dense forests survive inland. In the north, the forests contain deciduous (broadleaf) trees, such as oak. The guanacaste tree, also known as the elephant ear tree, spreads a wide and shady canopy. Tall cohune palm forests abound in the south, while mahogany and logwood have been valuable sources of income for centuries. In some areas, coniferous (cone-bearing) trees, including the Caribbean pine, grow in sandy soil. In the Maya Mountains, heavy rainfall and high humidity spur the growth of orchids and bromeliads (a family of tropical plants). The black orchid is the national flower.

Where the land meets the sea, mangroves grow in dense thickets. These plants have partly aboveground roots that thrive on brackish (salty), still water. Mangroves provide a sheltered habitat for a great variety of birdlife, fish, and marine animals. Fish such as tarpon, bonefish, barracudas, sharks, and marlins thrive in coastal waters. Manatees—large aquatic mammals sometimes called sea cows—swim here. Coastal areas and river mangroves are also home to many kinds of birds, including herons, storks, ibis, egrets, spoonbills, and gulls.

Off the coast of Belize lie coral reefs. Although a reef looks similar to stone, it is actually made up of tiny animals called corals. Corals live in large groups, or colonies. Because reefs contain valuable minerals and nutrients, they sustain varied and often colorful waterlife. Species swimming among Belize's reefs include damselfish, spiny lobster, and triggerfish.

The interior of Belize abounds in wildlife species that have grown rare in other parts of Central America. Wild turkeys, baboons, and wildcats called ocelots roam the western and southern forests. The jabiru stork of Belize is the largest flying bird in the Western Hemisphere. Owls emerge at night to hunt small creatures in the forests. Jaguars prowl the Cockscomb Basin Wildlife Sanctuary and Jaguar Preserve, the only jaguar reserve in the world. The national animal is the tapir. This plant-eating mammal resembles a pig with a short trunk. The tapir is an endangered species, as are howler monkeys and several other mammals native to Belize.

A jaguar in captivity relaxes. It is extremely rare to spot a jaguar in the wild. The Belizean government set aside 150 square miles (390 sq. km) of land as the Cockscomb Basin Wildlife Sanctuary and Jaguar Preserve. Approximately two hundred jaguars make this area home.

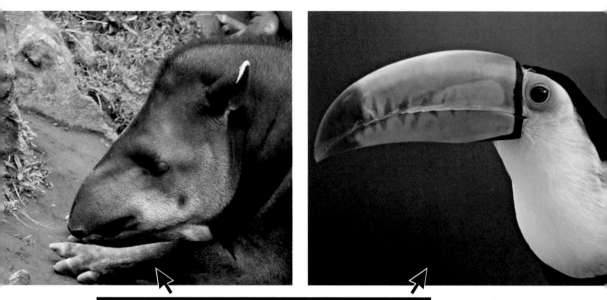

The tapir *(left)* **and the colorful keel-billed toucan** *(right)* are two of the unusual species that live in Belize.

The Belizean rain forest shelters hummingbirds, parrots, toucans, and vultures. Dangerous and poisonous snakes, including the boa constrictor, pit viper, coral snake, and rattlesnake, thrive in the rain forest and savanna regions. Iguanas and other reptiles also live in Belize.

Environmental Issues

A major environmental problem facing Belize is heavy deforestation, or loss of trees. As farmers move into new land, they clear trees and brush to make way for fields and pasture. The trees are used for firewood or sent to lumber mills. Without tree roots to anchor the soil, the bare land becomes vulnerable to flooding and erosion. The construction of new roads and towns also takes a toll on the natural environment.

The urban centers of Belize have problems as well. During heavy rains, sewage and industrial waste often contaminate the wells that people depend on for freshwater. Coastal cities have polluted nearby beaches and the sea with untreated sewage.

The coral reefs offshore suffer bleaching. Pollution or rising temperatures increase the ocean water's acid levels. This acidity "bleaches" corals, robbing them of their bright colors. In some places, bleaching kills the cor-

Visit www.vgsbooks.com for links to websites with additional information about Belize's environment.

This colony of brain coral shows signs of coral bleaching. Some scientists believe that coral bleaching is a result of rising ocean temperatures and more frequent storms, both attributed to global warming.

als altogether. In addition to being an environmental issue, coral bleaching represents a serious threat to Belize's tourist industry. Many tourists come to Belize to scuba dive and snorkel among the nation's colorful coral reefs.

Natural Resources

Belize has hardwood forests, fertile soil, and some mineral resources. There are small deposits of minerals useful in industry. These include bauxite (the raw material of aluminum), cassiterite (used to make tin), and limestone. Geologists are exploring the country and the coastal seabed in search of oil and natural gas. As of 2009, only a few small deposits had been found. The country's fast-flowing rivers hold the potential for hydropower projects, which harness the power of rushing water to create energy.

As a colony of Great Britain, Belize was an important source of timber. The colony cut and exported stands of logwood (used to make dyes) and mahogany. These resources gradually disappeared from regions where they were easy to reach. In the twenty-first century, Belize strictly controls the use of this resource to preserve its remaining natural forests and wildlife habitat.

Cities

About half of Belize's people live in urban areas. The nation has several important cities, as well as many small towns and villages.

BELIZE CITY, the largest urban center in the country, lies at the mouth of the Belize River. Belize City remains the cultural and economic center of the nation, although the modern capital is Belmopan. With a population of close to 64,000, Belize City remains a relatively small city, with few multistory buildings.

Haulover Creek, an extension of the Belize River, divides the city into northern and southern sections. The creek flows past the central business district and into the city's harbor. Northern Belize City is the site of the Fort George Lighthouse. The Fort George neighborhood was the site of the original settlement. It offers parks and walks along the harbor. Suburbs stretch along the Northern Highway and Western Highway, the main roads linking Belize City with the nation's interior.

The city traces its history to an old Mayan fishing village named Holzuz. British timber cutters settled there in the 1600s. These settlers raised Belize Town on the site. People also called this area the Bay Settlement. Sailors, pirates, and slaves from Jamaica, a British colony in the Caribbean, all lived here. Some came to work or to take part in the logging industry, and Belize grew as a center for the export of mahogany and logwood.

In 1892 the British named Belize Town (which later became known as Belize City) as the capital of their colony of British Honduras. But the low-lying city was vulnerable to storms and coastal flooding. Hurricanes devastated the city in the mid-twentieth century. One storm in 1961 prompted the government to move the capital to Belmopan. Belize City later gained a reputation for street crime and drug trafficking. In recent years, tourism and legal gambling have revived the city's fortunes. A new terminal for cruise ships will bring a greater number of tourists into the city.

SAN IGNACIO, with a population of 18,300, is the capital of Cayo District. It lies on the Macal River about 70 miles (113 km) southwest of Belize City. This town has a great variety of ethnic groups, including descendants of the ancient Maya, recent Chinese immigrants, and Lebanese families. The Hawksworth Bridge, the only suspension bridge in Belize, separates San Ignacio from its sister city, Santa Elena.

Vehicles and pedestrians make their way down a main road in Belize City.

BELMOPAN (population 16,400) has been the capital of Belize since 1970. Built 50 miles (80 km) southwest of Belize City, Belmopan lies in a flat plain near the Belize River. After Hurricane Hattie badly damaged Belize City in 1961, the national government selected Belmopan's site as a safer location for the country's capital city. The group chose Belmopan for its central location and its elevation out of the reach of tidal surges due to Caribbean storms. Construction began in 1967, and the national legislature began meeting in the city in 1970. The United States completed construction of its new embassy in Belmopan in 2006.

Belmopan includes a diverse population of Maya, Creoles (descendants of African slaves and European settlers), and Central American immigrants. A campus of the University of Belize lies in the city, as well as a small zone for industries and factories.

ORANGE WALK (population 16,000) is the capital of the Orange Walk District, in northwestern Belize. The original settlers of Orange Walk came from Mexico, where conflict in the 1840s drove many refugees into Central America. Although it grew as a market town and farming center, modern Orange Walk is also a center of Belizean tourism. Mayan ruins nestle in the surrounding forest, and plants and animals thrive in large wildlife sanctuaries nearby. Farmers in Orange Walk District grow sugarcane, citrus orchards, and soybeans. Legend says that the city's name came from the thick groves of orange trees that once grew along the town's riverbanks.

DANGRIGA (population 11,600) began in the early 1800s as a small logging settlement known as Stann Creek. It was the center of the Garinagu immigration of the nineteenth century. The Garinagu were former slaves from Saint Vincent, an island in the Caribbean Sea. They made this remote coast their home. The town was an important export center for Belizean citrus. It was also the last station on the only railroad line built in the colony, the Stann Creek Railway. Belizeans know the town best for its annual Settlement Day celebration. On November 19, Dangriga holds a big party, with dancing, drumming, and a canoe parade, to mark the historical arrival of the Garinagu in large dugout canoes.

COROZAL (population 9,100) lies in northern Belize near the border with Mexico. The first settlers of Corozal were Mexican refugees from Mexico's Yucatán Peninsula, which had violent social conflict during the nineteenth century. In 1955 Hurricane Janet roared through Corozal, destroying most of the town. The townspeople rebuilt their homes around a historic center, where visitors can still see the remains of an old fort and a lighthouse. The remains of a Mayan city known as Santa Rita lie on the outskirts of town. Archaeologists have yet to excavate this ancient ruin.

HISTORY AND GOVERNMENT

Humans began settling in Central America as early as ten thousand to fifteen thousand years ago. Archaeologists believe that the first inhabitants arrived from southeastern Mexico and Guatemala. Early Belize may also have had settlers from the islands of the Caribbean.

The earliest inhabitants hunted wild animals and gathered wild plants for food. They built small communities along the rivers and seacoast. Later, farmers settled forest clearings and raised corn, squash, and beans.

The Mayan Civilization

Archaeologists date the rise of the Maya to about 2500 B.C. The Mayan Empire eventually spread across the Yucatán Peninsula, northern Guatemala, and Belize. About 2000 B.C., the Maya were gathering in small cities, which served as market, craft, and trading centers. The settlement of Cuello, in northern Belize, rose around this time. It is the earliest known Mayan town.

Mayan farmers built irrigation systems to water their crops. They practiced slash-and-burn agriculture. They burned clearings out of the forest and farmed the soil until it was no longer fertile. They also developed the skills of pottery, metalworking, and creating jewelry from jade (a greenish stone) and other stones.

The Maya adopted cacao beans as their unit of currency. The Maya traded salt, fish, copper, honey, and precious stones such as jade and a natural form of black glass called obsidian. They built an extensive network of trails that linked Belize with the Yucatán Peninsula and Guatemala. Mayan merchants also traded along the seacoast and via the web of rivers that crisscross the region. The Belize River and the New River were once main highways of Mayan commerce.

The religion of the Maya was linked to their close observation of nature and the sky. They worshipped several deities, or divine beings, in human form or in the form of various animals. Itzamna was the creator, a god of fire and of the home. Kukulcan was a feathered snake. Chac was the god of storms and several jaguar gods reigned over the underworld. This dark realm contained the souls of all the dead.

The Classic Period

Historians divide Mayan history into several periods. The formative period began in about 1200 B.C. The Maya began to build large cities throughout Belize. A central palace and temple complex lay at the heart of each of these communities. The tallest monuments rose far above the tallest trees in the rain forest. At its peak, the Mayan realm in Belize was home to more than a million people.

The Maya developed a complex system of mathematics and astronomy. The priestly caste (social class) made regular observations of the sun, the moon, and the planets. A calendar marked time in several cycles of various lengths, including a solar year of 365 days. Seasonal rituals helped to coordinate planting and harvesting. Scribes carved important dates and events on stone slabs, many of which have survived. Archaeologists are still deciphering the pictographic symbols the Maya used to write their language.

> The Maya developed a complex calendar and a system of writing. They also invented a method of preserving their writings on stone slabs and on tree bark. Some of these writings—the first books in the Americas—have survived.

The Mayan civilization entered the classic period in about A.D. 250. In Belize the cities of Caracol and Altun Ha rose to become powerful city-states. These realms controlled land and dominated smaller communities. Mayan cities also rose on Ambergris Caye and other islands. The people of Lamanai built large temple pyramids. Smaller cities dotted the plains and forests, linked by a network of footpaths and river routes.

In Mayan cities, a priesthood and a caste of powerful families held control over trade and an army. Merchants belonged to another influential caste. Farmers in the surrounding countryside were a source of food and tribute (payments to the ruling classes). Rival cities often fought over trade and territory. Despite the frequent conflicts, the urban civilization of the Maya thrived for the next five hundred years.

Lamanai and Santa Rita were among the most powerful Mayan cities of Belize. Caracol carried on a long campaign against the gigantic city of Tikal, in northern Guatemala. The war ended in a large battle and a victory for Caracol in the seventh century A.D.

Mayan civilization began to decline in about the tenth century. Many cities fell into disrepair. The inhabitants of others abandoned their homes. Over the centuries, the surrounding rain forest buried hundreds of Mayan

Over time Belize's fast-growing jungles overtook many ancient Mayan buildings. Archaeologists have been working to uncover Mayan sites, such as this one in Caracol, to discover clues to the past.

towns in vines and undergrowth. Small farming communities survived in isolated forest clearings.

Archaeologists debate the causes of this decline. Overpopulation may have depleted the soil, leading to famine and civil conflict. A drought may have caused crops to fail. Trade goods may have become scarce.

Some Maya emigrated northward into the Yucatán. Those who remained returned to subsistence farming, growing only enough food to survive. Despite the general decline, the spoken Mayan language and some other parts of the culture, such as religious beliefs, survived. Several Mayan cities continued to thrive until a new civilization reached the shores of Belize in the 1400s.

◎ Explorers from Spain

By the end of the fifteenth century, European navigators were exploring the coasts of Central America. The Italian captain Christopher Columbus brought a small Spanish fleet to these waters in 1492. Another Spanish fleet encountered the Maya in the Gulf of Honduras in 1502. The Spanish navigators were seeking gold and trade routes between the Americas and Europe.

But the foreigners sailed the Caribbean waters with great caution. The offshore reefs and cayes of Belize posed a danger to ships. The coasts of Belize held other obstacles, such as low-lying marshes and mangroves, which made exploration and settlement difficult. In addition, the indigenous population was sparse, offering few trade goods and no gold.

THE SPANISH PRISONER

One of the first Europeans to set foot in Belize was a Spanish castaway, Gonzalo Guerrero. Captured by the Maya in 1511, he made a new life in Central America. He married the daughter of a Mayan chief, Nachankan, and had three children— Belize's first mestizos (people with Native American and European ancestors).

In 1511 a Spanish ship ran aground on a reef in the waters off northern Belize. A group of Maya captured the shipwrecked sailors and took them prisoner. This was the first time Europeans set foot on Belizean territory.

By this time, the Mayan calendar and written language had long fallen out of use. The scattered Mayan communities had few weapons. The Maya did not cooperate with one another to resist the outsiders and had no defense against the guns and cannons of the Europeans.

As a result, the Spanish dominated the Maya. During the sixteenth century, Spanish forces conquered Mayan cities in the Yucatán Peninsula and northern Belize. The most powerful weapon that the Spanish carried was disease. The Maya had no natural resistance to smallpox and other deadly plagues. Entire cities disappeared as the people sickened and died.

At this time, Spanish missionaries (religious workers) were landing as well. Their goal was to convert the indigenous people to Christianity, the dominant faith in Europe. Missionaries raised the first Christian church in Belize at Lamanai about 1570. In 1618 the Spanish raised another mission at the ancient city of Tipu, where Mayan families were still living.

For several decades, Maya under Spain's rule in the Yucatán had also been fleeing into Tipu and northern Belize, far from the main sea and river routes. The Spanish governors of Mexico had trouble controlling this isolated region. Beginning in 1638, the people of Tipu rebelled against Spanish control. Soon a full-scale revolt had spread to all northern Belize.

The Baymen

The Spanish had another opponent to face—British pirates. Also called buccaneers, these outlaws found the islands off Belize an ideal place to ambush passing ships. Buccaneers raided Spanish ships for the gold and other goods they were carrying from various parts of the region. Many buccaneers took shelter from pursuit in the bays along the Belizean seacoast.

The buccaneers became the first British settlers in Belize. They set up small camps and trading posts, known as stands, along the coast. They cut logwood for export. This wood was a source of dye that wool factories in England used. The Spanish king granted the timber cutters the legal right to settle. But the Spanish still claimed authority over all Central America.

This illustration shows **pirates attacking Spanish ships** in 1669. It was published in a book called *The Buccaneers of America* by John Esquemeling. Esquemeling himself was a pirate with Captain Henry Morgan.

A Scottish sea captain named Peter Wallace established a small settlement in central Belize in 1638. Wallace was a privateer, a sailor granted permission by the British king to raid the ships and settlements of the Spanish. Privateers also looted stray vessels that had wrecked along the shores. The British sailors and settlers earned the nickname Baymen, after their settlement, the Bay of Honduras. The Bay Settlement gained a reputation as the home of dangerous and violent ruffians.

In the meantime, Britain challenged Spain in the western Caribbean. A British fleet captured the last Spanish outpost on the island of Jamaica in 1655. From this base, the British sent out privateers to capture Spanish cargoes. British ships sailed the Caribbean coast from the Yucatán south to Belize and Honduras.

The Bay Settlement remained well outside of British and Spanish authority. The governor of Jamaica had formal control of British claims in Central America. But Britain did not bother to organize a colony in the Bay Settlement. The settlers ruled their own affairs. In 1670 Britain and Spain signed an agreement that formally allowed British settlers in Belize.

The Spanish still sought control over the profitable logwood trade. From time to time, Spanish soldiers raided the British settlements. But after fighting destructive wars on the European continent, Spain's influence in the Caribbean was waning. In 1713 the European powers signed the Treaty of Utrecht. Following this agreement, Spain no longer had exclusive rights to trade in Central America. For example, the treaty granted the South Sea Company, a British firm, the right to transport goods between Britain and the Americas. The company also began to supply African slaves to the Bay Settlement.

But Spanish raids on the Bay Settlement continued. The governor of Yucatán—then controlled by Spain—organized a raid in 1733. A large fleet and several hundred soldiers sailed into Belizean waters. The raiders stormed ashore and burned homes, ships, docks, and warehouses. The settlers scattered into the forest, only to return and rebuild. In Belize Town, the loggers built a fort to resist these attacks.

In 1756 a war broke out in Europe. The Seven Years' War (1756–1763) ended with the Treaty of Paris in 1763. This agreement allowed the British to trade logwood from Central America. But it also granted Spain authority over the region.

A Spanish force from the Yucatán arrived in Belize in 1779. The attack drove the British out for several years. By the Convention of London, a 1786 treaty, Spain allowed the Baymen to continue their export of logwood and mahogany. In the same agreement, Britain again confirmed Spanish rule in Central America.

In the summer of 1798, the Spanish sent another fleet from Mexico to conquer the British settlements in Central America. In September the British and Spanish skirmished among the offshore cayes. This Battle of Saint George's Caye drove the Spanish away, permanently ending Spain's claim to Belize. In the 1820s, Spain also lost control of Mexico and the rest of Central America, where the colonies of Spain won their independence.

The Timber Economy

Through the early nineteenth century, logwood remained the Bay Settlement's most important export. Loggers set up their camps near rivers and streams. The Belizean rivers made it easy to transport their cut logwood downstream to the coast.

But with a plentiful supply, the prices for this resource were low. Eventually, European textile makers created artificial dyes. These lowered the demand for Central American logwood, and the settlement turned to mahogany. There were thick stands of mahogany growing on the plains. This hardwood was in high demand in Europe and North America. Furniture makers, carpenters, and shipbuilders all used mahogany. To exploit this resource, investors bought large parcels of land in the Bay Settlement. They set up mahogany-cutting camps. Settlers built new towns in the interior.

Mahogany became the mainstay of trade. But mahogany cutters gradually depleted this resource. New trees required many years to mature. Loggers had to move farther inland to find new stands. This drove up costs of production and transportation.

Meanwhile, farmers also planted stands of citrus, banana, and sugarcane. But growers faced many difficulties. The British government heavily taxed exports from the colony. This made the colony's products more expensive and, in turn, hurt demand for them.

British Honduras

In 1823 the Garinagu people arrived in Central America. The Garinagu were descendents of slaves, originally from West Africa, and native Arawak and Carib peoples. The Garinagu had worked in the British colony of Saint Vincent in the Caribbean. British planters on Saint Vincent, fearing that the Garinagu workers might rebel, expelled them. The Garinagu sailed across the Caribbean and eventually settled Stann Creek and other places in Belize. Many worked as timber cutters. Others grew fruits, sugarcane, and vegetables on small farms. Punta Gorda, in southern Belize, and Dangriga became centers of Garinagu settlement. The Garinagu lived apart from the Maya and from the British settlers. They had very limited legal rights in the colony. They could not purchase land or vote.

Meanwhile, important changes were taking place for the colony's slaves. In 1833 Great Britain officially abolished slavery in all British-held lands. The practice of slavery did not end overnight but gradually lessened. By 1838 most slaves in Belize had been freed. However, many of the freed slaves still depended on landowners and former slaveholders for work.

This illustrated children's book, called *The Black Man's Lament*, was written by a member of the British Anti-Slavery Society in 1826. The book describes the life of an African man who was captured by slave traders and sent to work on a sugar plantation in a Caribbean colony.

12   THE BLACK MAN'S LAMENT.

NEGROES HOLING THE CANE-FIELD.

As holes must all *at once* be made,
    Together we must work or stop ;

THE BLACK MAN'S LAMENT.   13

PLANTING.

When we have dug sufficient space,
    The bright-eye top* of many a cane,
Lengthways, we in the trenches place,
    And *then* we trenches dig again.

By the 1840s, Britain had established strong control over Belize, though it was not officially a colony. But the British government invested little money in the area. Instead, the British paid more attention to its colonies in Asia and Africa. Few settlers arrived in Belize from the British Isles. And the local economy struggled as the price of mahogany and logwood on the world market fell.

In 1854 Britain took steps toward setting up a colonial government in Belize. British officials established the office of superintendent and also created a legislative group called the Legislative Assembly. Only property owners had the right to run for election to this body, which had eighteen members. Residents without money or property could not vote. The superintendent, appointed by the British ruler, had the right to write new laws or reject those passed by the assembly.

At the same time, Guatemala was making claims to the territory of Belize. The Guatemalan government relied on Spain's longtime settlement and government of Central America. As a former part of the Spanish colonial empire, Guatemala believed it had a right to also govern Belize. Spanish rulers had accepted British settlement but had never formally recognized Britain's right to rule in Belize. The dispute still has not been completely resolved.

In 1862 the British government formally declared that Belize was a colony called British Honduras. In the meantime, the colony was attracting settlers from a variety of places. Many came from Mexico, due to a civil conflict in the Yucatán Peninsula. The Caste War (1847–1901) drove refugees across Mexico's border into British Honduras. Most Mayan arrivals settled in the town of San Pedro and the surrounding area. But the British administration did not allow the Maya to own land or vote.

During the 1860s, the American Civil War (1861–1865) broke out between the Union (Northern) and Confederate (Southern) regions of the United States. This event affected British Honduras. For example, the Confederacy used the colony as a source of timber, which boosted the colony's logging trade here. And when the war ended with

BARON BLISS

One of the most famous foreigners in Belize was Baron Henry Edward Ernest Victor Bliss. Baron Bliss died in 1926, and he willed his entire fortune to Belize—even though he had never actually set foot in the country. Too ill to come ashore, he lived on a yacht off the Belizean coast. But he came to appreciate the hospitality of fishers and other Belizeans who visited his boat. The country honors him each year with a national holiday—Baron Bliss Day—on March 9.

the defeat of the South, many Confederate refugees settled in British Honduras.

In the late 1800s, Scottish and Portuguese immigrants to British Honduras built the town of Placencia. This town became the center of a citrus-growing industry. The United Fruit Company, based in the United States, built the Stann Creek Railway to move fruit to harbors on the coast. This was the first and only railroad in British Honduras.

The Crown Colony

The Legislative Assembly saw the arrival of outsiders from Europe and North America as a threat to its authority. To combat this threat, the assembly sought closer ties to the British government. In the 1870s, the assembly asked for direct rule by Britain's Colonial Office. In April 1871, a new constitution organized Belize as a crown colony. A nine-member Legislative Council replaced the assembly. Instead of a superintendent, a lieutenant governor ruled British Honduras. The lieutenant governor had the right to appoint most members of the Legislative Council.

With foreigners buying up land in the south, the colony set aside some land in this region for the use of the Maya and the Garinagu. Meanwhile, British companies staked claims to large parcels of land in Belize. The largest firm was the Belize Estate and Produce Company. The company took its name from the Belize River. This and other overseas companies held control of the colony's forestry and trade. They also had representatives on the Legislative Council.

Few Belizean settlers had the means to compete for productive land and establish farms. Although British Honduras had plentiful fertile land, its agricultural sector developed very slowly. Settlement was sparse, and much of the land was reserved for timber production. The colony remained dependent on imported food and basic goods, such as construction material, machinery, and clothing.

Conflict over political and economic power simmered at the turn of the century. Underlying this conflict was rivalry over land and resources between recent immigrants from Europe and the Creoles. The Creoles had no representatives on the Legislative Council. In protest, they asked for elections for council seats. But the British did not want to see their appointed lieutenant governor lose authority. The British merchant companies also resisted any change in the constitution.

In 1914 World War I (1914–1918) broke out in Europe. Some residents of British Honduras fought alongside the British against Germany. Beyond this involvement, the conflict had little direct impact on the colony. But when Germany lost the war and Belizean soldiers returned, unrest broke out. Even after serving their colony in wartime, black soldiers still faced discrimination and fewer rights at home. They rioted in 1919 to protest this treatment. Known as the Ex-Servicemen's Riot, this protest was put down by colonial forces. But the former soldiers did not give up in their fight for fair treatment. One soldier, Samuel Alfred Haynes, worked to organize a local branch of the Universal Negro Improvement Association.

In the meantime, the economy of the colony slowed down. British Honduras competed with many other colonies exporting mahogany in the Americas and eastern Asia. Little of the colony's land was farmed, and the transportation system remained primitive. British Honduras did take part in a busy market in chicle, however. This resin, or gum, harvested from the sapodilla tree, went into chewing gum. Export of chicle to the United States made several landowning families wealthy.

Through the 1920s, British Honduras remained an underdeveloped colony. Logging and chicle harvesting provided nearly all export goods. To reach remote stands of mahogany, however, logging companies had to cut roads through the western forests and mountains. The expenses of logging rose, and the economic benefits of harvesting timber fell.

At the same time, the grip of British companies on the administration began to weaken. Creole representatives began sitting on the Legislative Council. Several Creole families were growing wealthy through trade with the United

THE CRYSTAL SKULL: A HOAX?

In 1926 Anna Mitchell-Hedges, the adopted daughter of explorer F. A. Mitchell-Hedges, was exploring Lubaantun. At this ancient Mayan site, Anna discovered a strange object underneath an altar. She found a huge globe of quartz crystal carved into the shape of a human skull (*below*). The skull was a weapon of Mayan priests and had the power to kill—or so claimed Anna's father. He described the skull in his book *Danger My Ally*, which appeared in the 1950s.

Many people claim the discovery is a hoax. They believe they have evidence proving that German gem cutters made the "skull of doom" in the nineteenth century. Anna Mitchell-Hedges, who died in 2007 at the age of one hundred, didn't let anyone in on the secret.

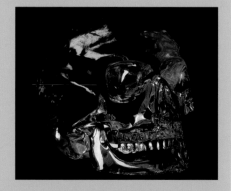

States. During the era of U.S. Prohibition (a ban on alcohol from 1920 to 1933), for example, some Creoles in Belize earned money by shipping liquor into the United States illegally.

The British governor of the colony resisted open elections (elections in which all eligible voters were allowed to take part freely) or any lessening of his authority. In the 1920s, the British government proposed holding elections for the Legislative Council, as long as the lieutenant governor kept "reserve powers." This would allow the lieutenant governor to dictate policy and new laws without the permission of the Legislative Council. The council rejected this stand. The demand for open elections continued.

Labor Troubles

A stock market crash in 1929 in the United States had dire effects in British Honduras. Exports slowed and foreign investment nearly stopped altogether. Then, in 1931, a devastating hurricane struck the coast of Belize. The hurricane leveled entire neighborhoods in Belize Town. Inland, the storm damaged farmland and orchards.

After this event, the economy of British Honduras went into a steep decline. During the same period, a sharp economic slowdown, called the Great Depression, was causing mass unemployment in the United States and Europe. Exports to the United States slowed, and many workers in British Honduras lost their livelihoods. Others were

In 1931 a hurricane destroyed towns and cities on the coast of Belize. The destruction, combined with an already weak economy, led to civil unrest in the country.

subject to low pay and harsh working conditions. Timber cutters and railroad workers staged violent protests.

In 1934 a large group of unemployed workers staged a protest in Belize Town. The governor responded with an offer of public works and a food ration. After the unrest began to die down, a lawyer named Antonio Soberanis Gómez helped found the Labourers and Unemployed Association (LUA). The group demanded unemployment benefits and a law establishing a minimum wage for workers.

The labor trouble pressured the colonial government to provide political change. The Legislative Council passed a new constitution in 1935. The colony still permitted only well-off property owners to vote. Nevertheless, several new political parties formed to press for further change. In 1941 the colony legalized trade unions (workers' associations). In 1943 labor leaders established the General Workers' Union to press for improved working conditions.

In the meantime, the border conflict with Guatemala was still brewing. In 1945 Guatemala drew up a new constitution. In this document, the territory of British Honduras was declared to be a part of Guatemala. From time to time, Guatemala massed its armed forces on the border. The British responded by holding naval maneuvers in the western Caribbean as a show of strength.

A New Party for Independence

In 1950 the People's United Party (PUP) formed. Its leaders came from the ranks of labor organizers. One of these leaders was George Cadle Price. Price was a member of the Belize Town Council. He also supported independence for British Honduras. His movement gathered strength on economic issues. Unemployment and poverty affected many Belizeans. Price inflation made many basic goods and food expensive. Most of the country's middle-class and working-class people supported PUP candidates. Those allowed to vote elected PUP members for seats on town councils.

The PUP also protested the strict voting laws, which prevented most Belizeans of having any say in political affairs. PUP leaders demanded that voters have the right to elect all members of the Legislative Council, rather than having the colonial administration appointing several members. To set out the legal rights and status of the colonists, the PUP demanded a new constitution. Price and other PUP leaders wanted to reduce the powers of the British-appointed lieutenant governor.

These efforts finally bore fruit in 1954. The colony wrote a new constitution, which created an assembly of elected representatives. The constitution also legalized voting for all adults who could read and write.

Citizens of British Honduras turn out to vote in the 1954 elections, in which women were allowed to vote for the first time. The People's United Party won a decisive victory.

In elections held in 1954, the PUP won 66 percent of the popular vote. PUP leaders won eight of nine seats in the new Legislative Assembly. The office of governor, appointed by the British government, began to lose its authority.

In 1958 the first Mennonites arrived in northern Belize. Mennonites are a religious group with their roots in sixteenth-century Netherlands. These tight-knit Christian communities were seeking fertile land and a place to follow their traditional farming and living customs. Many of them came from Canada.

From Colony to Nation

In 1961 another powerful storm, Hurricane Hattie, struck British Honduras. This hurricane convinced the colonial government to move the capital to higher ground. A new city began to rise on the site of Belmopan.

Meanwhile, some Belizeans continued to push for independence. British leaders were becoming more open to this idea. Britain had already granted independence to many of its other colonies, due partly to the effects of World War II and to a general trend away from colonialism and empire. In 1964 Britain granted sovereignty to the colony. This change meant that locally elected representatives and the prime minister ran the government, the military, and relations with foreign countries. British Honduras, however, was still a part of the British Commonwealth, an association of former British colonies. In the next year, the colony established a bicameral (two-house) legislature.

The colony still faced a claim by its western neighbor, Guatemala. The British authorities did not want to grant British Honduras full independence as long as Guatemala was threatening to invade. The

British feared becoming involved in a war between the two states. Meetings between the leaders of Guatemala and representatives from British Honduras did not solve the dispute.

To solve the problem, Britain and Guatemala agreed to have the United States propose a treaty. The proposed agreement, however, granted Guatemala extensive authority in British Honduras. Britain and British Honduras rejected the proposal, and tensions remained high. Guatemala gathered its troops along the border, and British navy ships appeared offshore. The British also stationed troops to discourage a Guatemalan invasion.

Even as talks with Guatemala stalled, the drive for independence rolled on. In July 1973, with both the British and the Belizeans seeing the colony's independence on the horizon, British Honduras's name changed to Belize. Belize still did not enjoy full independence. But its leaders gained the authority to dispute Guatemala's claim on their own. Belizean representatives met with the diplomats of other countries. They also appeared at the United Nations (UN), an international diplomatic organization, to press for full independence.

These efforts gained the support of Cuba, a Caribbean nation, and several Central American countries. Nicaragua, Panama, and Mexico all supported Belizean independence and opposed Guatemala's claims. In 1980 a vote in the UN officially demanded Belizean independence.

The diplomatic pressure finally convinced Britain to grant Belize full independence on September 21, 1981. Its head of state, officially, remained the monarch of Britain, Queen Elizabeth II. Belize also remained a member of the British Commonwealth. And with

On September 21, 1981, **Belizean prime minister George Price (*left at lectern*)** of the PUP accepted a handover of power from Prince Michael of Kent (*right*), who was representing his cousin, Queen Elizabeth II. Price became the leader of a newly independent Belize.

Guatemala still refusing to recognize Belize as a nation, more than one thousand British troops stayed to guard Belize against possible attacks. But the British colonial administration came to an end, and Belize became a free and independent nation. Its first prime minister was PUP leader George Cadle Price.

While Belizeans celebrated this new independence, disagreements arose among PUP leaders. These internal tensions weakened the party, which began to lose popularity. Opponents formed a rival party, the United Democratic Party (UDP), to dispute control of the government. The UDP defeated the PUP in the 1984 elections. Manuel Esquivel, leader of the UDP, became prime minister. Esquivel and the UDP lost to Price and the PUP in 1989.

The long dispute with Guatemala continued. The leaders of Guatemala still made claims that Belize legally belonged to their country. They sought control of Belize's Caribbean ports and trade.

In 1991, however, Guatemala finally recognized the independent and sovereign state of Belize. Guatemala and Belize signed a peace agreement in April 1993. Each country pledged not to invade the other. From time to time, the two countries continued to squabble over the precise location of their border.

> Visit www.vgsbooks.com for links to websites with additional information about Belize's independence from Great Britain.

Party Politics and Thorny Problems

In the early 1990s, Belize was enjoying economic growth. The country was bringing in foreign investment and a rising tide of visitors. Confident of victory, Price and the PUP called for elections in 1993. According to the constitution, the party in power can hold elections before the normal time (five years) has passed. If they win, they can serve another five years before the next election must be held. The UDP gained a surprise victory in the 1993 elections. Esquivel returned as prime minister.

While in office, the UDP leaders faced a scandal over immigration. Newspapers charged that the government ministers were selling falsified immigration permits. The UDP also lost favor over a new value added tax (VAT) that made the prices of many ordinary goods rise sharply.

George Cadle Price retired from politics in 1996. His successor as PUP leader was Said Musa. Musa and the PUP won election in 1998, when Musa became prime minister. During this administration, the government repealed (canceled) the VAT. Another PUP win in 2003 kept Musa in office. Musa became the first Belizean prime minister to hold office two terms in a row.

Meanwhile, the nation and its leaders dealt with a variety of social and environmental challenges. One troubling issue is crime. Drug traffickers in Belize ship illegal narcotics into the United States. The drug trade also leads to violent crime. Human trafficking is another problem in Belize. Human trafficking is the movement of people to exploit them in some way, usually by forcing them into labor or prostitution. In Belize, men, women, and children are trafficked, both from within the country and across borders. National leaders have pledged to end human trafficking, but this goal is not yet within sight.

Another social challenge involves land use for indigenous Belizeans. A controversy over land use went all the way to the Supreme Court of Belize. In October 2007, the court recognized the right of the Maya to keep mining, farming, and fishing rights on their ancestral lands. The ruling prohibited logging or mining by outsiders.

The health of the nation's valuable coral reefs is also a concern. Corals are a precious natural resource. They help support biodiversity. The barrier reef also helps protect Belize's islands and coast from hurricane surges. But coral bleaching harms more than the environment. Many Belizeans depend on tourism for their livelihood, and many tourists come to Belize to experience coral diving.

Elections in 2008 showed that many Belizeans were ready for a change in their country's government. The PUP's long period as the leading political party drew criticism. The party faced charges of corruption. Many voters were also unhappy with tax increases and rising prices. They elected UDP leader Dean Barrow to succeed Said Musa as prime minister.

Barrow, the first black prime minister in Belizean history, also holds the post of minister of finance. Belize is going through a period of rapid growth and investment by foreigners. This growth

United Democratic Party candidate **Dean Barrow** won the election in 2008. He is the country's first prime minister of African descent.

is causing a rise in prices on goods for ordinary citizens and damage to the country's fragile natural environment. The government is attempting to keep this growth under control.

◉ Government

The government of Belize is modeled on the parliamentary system of Britain. It is a democracy but still has a symbolic monarch—the queen of Great Britain, Elizabeth II. While she is the official head of government, she has very little power or influence on Belize's governance. Another official dating back to the colonial administration is the governor-general. The British monarch appoints this person, who acts as the crown's representative. The governor-general serves mainly as an adviser and British diplomat.

The real head of Belize's government and its executive branch is the prime minister. The governor-general also appoints the prime minister by choosing a member of the House of Representatives who is part of the political party with a majority in the House. With the advice of the prime minister, the governor-general appoints a cabinet. This group of advisers assists the prime minister. Its members oversee specific areas of government such as education, health care, and environmental issues.

While Belizean voters do not directly elect the prime minister, they do elect the House of Representatives, and therefore, they elect the candidates for prime minister. Every five years, voters choose the thirty-one members of the House.

The House is one part of Belize's National Assembly, a bicameral legislature. The other part is the twelve-person Senate. The prime minister, governor-general, and several other officials each appoint some of the Senate members. Like House members, Senate members serve five-year terms.

Belize consists of six districts, including Corozal, Orange Walk, Belize, Cayo, Stann Creek, and Toledo. District councils pass local ordinances. Mayors and village councils, elected by local residents, govern the cities and towns.

Each of these districts also has its own criminal and civil courts. The Supreme Court hears cases of national importance. Decisions of this court can be appealed by taking them to a national Court of Appeals. The governor-general appoints judges to these courts, in some cases with the advice of the prime minister.

THE PEOPLE

With a population of about 300,000, Belize is one of the least crowded nations in the world. The population density is about 36 people per square mile (14 per sq. km), far lower than any other country in Central America. The immigration rate, however, is high. Belize is attracting 10 new residents for every 1,000 persons already in the country. These newcomers come from Central America, North America, and Europe. Some are escaping poverty and seeking jobs. Others want to establish a second home in the tropics.

Immigration is having an effect on Belizean society. New arrivals from wealthier countries are building homes and vacation residences. This puts a strain on available resources, such as roads and public water supplies. Farmers and laborers who move to the Belizean towns seek housing, jobs, health care, and education for their children. This rising demand spreads the available facilities and resources very thin. The country's poverty rate stands at about 30 percent, with the highest rate in the Toledo District.

▶ Ethnic Groups

The small population of modern Belize includes several different ethnic groups. The earliest inhabitants, the Maya, have survived with their own language and culture. Later settlers from Europe, Central America, North America, Africa, and the Caribbean also contributed to the mix.

The mestizo population makes up about 50 percent of the population of modern Belize. Mestizos have a mixed ancestry of European and Native American ancestors. Most have family roots in the Mayan population. Many mestizos arrived in northern Belize from the Yucatán Caste War during the late 1800s. In more recent times, mestizos immigrated to Belize from Guatemala. In northern Belize, mestizos are in the majority.

The Creole group claims about 25 percent of the population. Creoles trace their ancestry to Africans who began arriving in Belize in the eighteenth century. Some of these ancestors were slaves. Others

These kids of Mayan descent live in a town in western Belize near the border with Guatemala.

settled in the country freely as timber cutters or farmers. They inter-married with Europeans. The result was a new language known as Kriol and distinct traditions of clothing and food. Creoles make up more than half the population of Belize City.

The Maya survived the arrival of Europeans in the sixteenth century. Many still live in small villages in Belize and work the land for a living. The largest concentration of Maya lives in southern Belize. The Maya divide themselves into several smaller groups, including Yucatec (in the north) and Kekchi and Mopan (in the west and south). About 11 percent of Belize residents claim Mayan ancestry and speak Mayan dialects (language variations).

The Garinagu, also known as the Garifuna, trace their roots to a group of African slaves who lived on the island of Saint Vincent in the early

This Garinagu schoolgirl from the Stann Creek District in eastern Belize wears traditional clothing, which reflects her African ancestry.

seventeenth century. These people intermarried with indigenous Carib and Arawak people. Seeing them as troublemakers, the governor of Saint Vincent expelled the Garinagu. The group then journeyed west to the shores of Central America. Many settled in Belize, where they make up about 6 percent of the modern population. Garinagu also live in Guatemala and Honduras. In the late twentieth century, many Garinagu emigrated from Central America to the U.S. cities of New York and Los Angeles in search of a better standard of living.

Several other ethnic groups live in Belize. These groups together comprise 8 percent of Belizeans. One of the fastest growing communities is from nearby Central American countries. Many immigrants arrive from Guatemala, Honduras, and other Central American neighbors. These Spanish speakers seek out jobs in the cities or claim new land to farm in the countryside. Belize also has many residents who visited as tourists and then made a permanent home in the country. These include people from the United States, Canada, Britain, and several European countries.

CHINA ARRIVES IN BELIZE

Chinese immigrants have long been coming to Central America and especially Belize. Many came seeking jobs and better lives than they had in China. The sparsely populated colony of British Honduras welcomed them. During World War II, when China fought Japan, more Chinese left to escape Japan's occupation of their homeland. Many settled in Belize City. A significant population of Chinese Belizeans live in the town of San Ignacio in west central Belize.

◗ Health

Belize has taken major steps in eradicating tropical diseases such as yellow fever and dengue fever, a virus transmitted by mosquitoes that causes high fever, severe headaches, and muscle and joint pain. Malaria, carried by the anopheles mosquito, remains a threat in rural and forested areas. Waterborne diseases such as cholera and dysentery are present in areas where the public water source is a local river or well and sanitary systems are lacking. Filth flows into the drinking water, spreading disease.

Belize has a national system of health insurance and public health facilities. The average life expectancy in Belize is 73 years (71 years for men, and 74 for women). This figure is one year lower than the average life expectancy in Central America. Belize City has the best medical facilities in the country and most of the country's doctors. In the countryside, clinics provide care for the sick and vaccinations for the young. Some rural communities have very limited health facilities and few

A patient with an eye infection is treated with cactus sap. People in rural areas often turn to traditional medicine for common ailments.

doctors or nurses. People in these areas often rely on traditional medicines, made from tropical plants and flowers, to heal sickness or care for injuries.

High blood pressure, heart disease, and diabetes are growing problems in urban areas. Pregnant women often suffer complications during childbirth, due to a lack of prenatal (before birth) care. Nevertheless, Belize reduced its infant mortality rate from 35 per 1,000 live births in 1990 to 16 per 1,000 in 2006. This rate, which is higher in poorer rural areas, is lower than the average figure for the Central American region.

Belize is also struggling with HIV (human immunodeficiency virus). This virus causes acquired immunodeficiency syndrome, or AIDS. The incidence of HIV has been increasing since the early 1990s, when statistics on the disease were first kept. In 2008 about 2 percent of the population between the ages of fifteen and forty-nine carried the virus, the highest rate in the region. The government has begun a program of free testing as well as treatment for HIV-infected people.

Education

Its history as a British colony left Belize with the basic framework of British schooling. The Church of England (a Christian faith based in England) built many small private schools. Baptists and Roman Catholics founded many others. In modern times, church schools still account for most primary education. The government helps run these schools and pays teachers' salaries. In some remote areas, small church schools still provide the only means of primary education.

By law, Belizean students are supposed to attend primary school for eight years. Not all families in Belize send their children to school for the entire time, however. In rural areas, it is common for young people to attend only a few years of school, to learn the basics of reading and writing. They then leave early to help their families farm and do other daily jobs. Only about half of all school-age children in Belize complete primary studies.

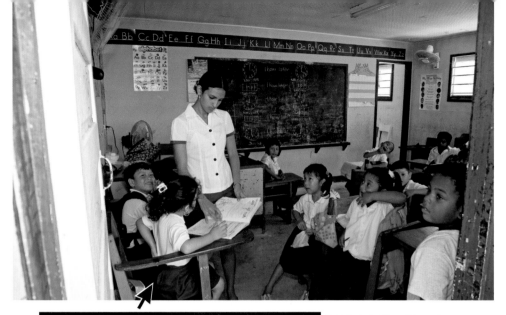

Students in a primary school in western Belize receive instruction from their teacher. The Belizean government sees that all young children have access to free education.

The nation's literacy rate (the number of people who can read and write) varies from 75 to 90 percent, depending on the district. The highest literacy rates are in Belize City and other cities that have most of their children attending school.

After completing primary school, students may opt for a four-year course in secondary school. To pass to a higher grade, they must pass a year-end examination. Public schools emphasize vocational or technical courses. These classes train and prepare students for specific occupations. Private schools offer more academic courses, which prepare the student for higher education.

The government of Belize founded the University of Belize in 1986. This school's main campus is in Belize City. There are smaller campuses in Belmopan, Toledo, and around the country. For example, agriculture students study at the Central Farm Campus in the Cayo District. The university's Institute of Marine Studies has field stations on several islands.

Other institutes of higher education in Belize include the Belize School of Nursing, located in Belize City. There are several private medical colleges in Belize as well. These schools train hopeful doctors from several foreign nations, including the United States.

MEDICAL SCHOOL IN BELIZE

There are several schools of medicine in Belize. These schools welcome many of their students from North America. Some of the schools are quite small. The Medical University of the Americas, on Ambergris Caye, has only fifty students. These schools offer medical training similar in quality to schools in the United States, at a lower cost and with smaller classes.

Women and Families

Belizean women face an uphill struggle to achieve social and economic equality with men. The country has few female legislators or government ministers. Women also have a difficult time entering professions and skilled trades. A clause in the Belizean constitution guarantees equal pay for equal work. Nevertheless, many women find themselves earning less than men who perform the same job.

In many families, women are expected to remain home, where their primary role is tending to the house and children. Belize, like many Caribbean nations, has a high percentage of female-headed households. Sometimes this situation occurs because fathers leave the family home to find work. In other cases, couples simply do not stay together. Many children in Belize are born to single mothers. Most female-headed households live at or below the poverty line, which stands at an annual income of about $1,300. Even for mothers who work, the pay is generally low and child care is scarce.

In schools, pregnant teenagers are expelled from school. Poor prenatal health care also leads to a high rate of infections and birth complications. Especially among the Maya and in rural areas generally, a lack of doctors and clinics affects the health of mothers and their babies.

Domestic violence is also a problem in Belize. Women who are victims of violence at home seldom make a report to the police.

Traditionally, the primary role of women in Belize has been to raise a family.
While many Belizeans would like to see more gender equality between women and men, progress is slow. Women received the right to vote as recently as 1954. For comparison, women in the United States could legally vote in 1920.

The police lack training in dealing with such cases, and there is only one women's shelter in the entire country, in Belize City.

City and Country Life

About half the population of Belize lives in cities and towns. Most of the country's recent immigrants have moved into cities. In urban areas, more jobs are available. Many new arrivals work at basic labor jobs. Others drive taxis or sell food, clothing, and other goods on the streets. Service industries such as banking and real estate, tourist services, and government service have brought people into the middle class.

In rural areas and small towns, many Belizeans live among large, extended families. One household may include children, parents, grandparents, aunts, and uncles. Family ties are close, and most Belizeans keep in touch with a large circle of friends and family.

Cities are made up of single- or double-story private homes. The traditional urban home is made of wood planks. Some families paint their homes in bright colors. A thick layer of paint protects the wood from moisture and decay. A veranda or balcony allows people to sit outside in the evening, a favorite pastime. Many homes near the seacoast are built on stilts or pilings. This allows them to avoid flooding during heavy storms. In the countryside, some homes are made of palm fronds or adobe (dried mud bricks). Many rural families live in small homes of one or two rooms, with a living and sleeping area divided from a kitchen. Rural families spend more of their time outdoors, whether they are working or at leisure.

The Maya of Belize have survived centuries of settlement and occupation by outsiders. Mayan families live in small villages and build their homes of adobe, thatch, or brick and block. Most live by subsistence farming, hunting and fishing, and making traditional crafts and other goods.

Visit www.vgsbooks.com for links to websites with additional information and statistics about Belize.

CULTURAL LIFE

The people of Belize have a varied cultural background. No single nation or ethnic group has dominated the country's history. Many immigrants have come from foreign lands, including Mexico, Central America, Europe, Africa, and the islands of the Caribbean region. Chinese, Indian, and Lebanese families call Belize home, with many still making everyday use of their own languages and customs.

As a result, the small nation of Belize has a range of literature, art, and music that is greater than that of some nations many times its size. But Belizean artists are still identified primarily with the ethnic group to which they belong. Musicians of Garinagu or Creole descent, for example, frequently have musical styles that reflect this heritage. Writers may describe the experiences unique to mestizos. Mayan crafts have distinct patterns and motifs. Because of many different outlooks, this young country has yet to bring forth a Belizean national style.

Languages and Literature

As a British colony, Belize adopted English as its official language. Most people in Belize can read and speak English, although most do not use it as a first language. In public schools, textbooks and instruction are in English. This can be a problem for students who don't speak English at home but instead use Spanish or Kriol, a mixture of vocabulary from English and from African languages.

In most of Belize, Kriol is the most common form of everyday communication. Most Belizeans know many Kriol words, no matter what ethnic group they belong to. This language varies throughout the country, with unique phrases used in certain regions.

Spanish is the language of immigrants from Mexico and Central America. Most of the people in northern Belize speak Spanish as their first language. But in the streets of San Ignacio, people also use English, Chinese, and Marathi (a language that arrived with immigrants from India). Most Mennonite families, who live in

SOME KRIOL WORDS

chinchi	a very small amount
tideh	today
vex	angry
gwaana	iguana
hooyu	owl
taapong	tarpon (a kind of fish)
waari	wild pig
wowla	boa constrictor

more isolated rural regions, speak Plautdietsch. This language, sometimes called Mennonite German, is an old German dialect that is also related to Dutch. Some Belizean Mennonites also speak English.

Mayan people speak several dialects. Mopan and Kekchi are commonly heard in western Belize. The Maya of northern Belize use Yucatec. The Garinagu people speak Garifuna, a language with roots in Native American languages of the Caribbean, including Carib and Arawak. Garifuna and similar languages have mostly died out in the islands of the Caribbean region but still thrive in Belize, Honduras, and Nicaragua.

English is the primary language of Belizean writers, poets, and journalists. Zee Edgell has published her works in Europe and the United States. *Beka Lamb*, her first novel, appeared in 1982. The book describes the friendship of two school friends who must deal with the tough—and sometimes unfair—problems facing many Belizean girls. This book was the first Belizean literary work to win widespread fame outside of the country. Edgell's stories have been translated from English into several languages.

This sign says, "We are Garinagu today, tomorrow, forever," in the Garifuna language. Garifuna is one of several languages spoken in Belize.

Many Belizean writers take an active part in politics, either as elected leaders or journalists. Assad Shoman is a well-known Belizean writer and political figure. He has written a history of Belize as well as works on the country's politics and foreign relations. Evan X Hyde, the editor of the newspaper *Amandala*, writes regularly for print media and radio broadcasts. His *Knocking Our Own Ting* is a satire on the Battle of Saint George's Caye. Although this event is an important part of Belizean history, Hyde treats it as an event that worsened ethnic divisions among the settlers of Belize.

Art

Archaeologists have uncovered only a portion of the art and architecture created by the ancient Maya of Belize. Ruins and artifacts show a people skilled in sculpture, stonecutting, and jewelry making. Mayan artists employed figures of the gods, embodied in human form and in animals such as the jaguar.

At the site of Altun Ha, Mayan builders carefully sited and raised limestone temples on hilltops. The leaders of the city were buried with a wealth of artifacts, including jade and obsidian tools and ornaments. One grave held an enormous head made of jade. This mask of the sun god Kinich Ahau is the largest such piece ever found.

The Maya of modern Belize still craft household goods and jewelry. Small workshops in the Mayan heartland of southern Belize produce wool rugs and clothing, pottery, baskets woven from sisal and palm, hammocks, sandals, hats, and cotton dresses. Stone carvers carry on the ancient art of carving in stone and jade.

A Mayan woman weaves a brilliantly colored rug using the tools and techniques of her ancient Mayan ancestors.

This painting by Pen Cayetano depicts the Garinagu ceremony of Beluria. This nine-day celebration takes place when a loved one dies. Family members and friends mourn for nine days, ending with a final day of feasting, music, and dancing.

The art scene in modern Belize is as varied as the country's social and ethnic mixture. The painter Pen Cayetano, a self-taught Garinagu artist, has lived abroad for many years, making Belizean culture familiar in foreign lands through artwork as well as music. The artist Benjamin Nicholas illustrates daily life and work of the Garinagu people in his oil paintings. He studied in Guatemala and has since exhibited his works in Belize and in the United States. Angela Gegg has shown her paintings throughout Central America and the Caribbean. She has written a book and also appears as the host of a Belizean cooking show.

Music

Many different strands of Caribbean, Latin, and African music have combined in the music of modern Belize. The Creoles of Belize have an entire family of distinctive musical styles. *Brukdown*, a Creole folk music, originated in work and field songs of nineteenth-century loggers. These workers often sang tunes while working or while at rest. They later added instruments and adopted the rhythms of calypso, a Caribbean style. Brukdown performers sing and play guitars, marimbas (a percussion instrument made of wooden keys), and drums. Brukdown can be heard on the radio and in the streets. Accordionist Wilfred Peters leads the Boom and Chime Band, a popular brukdown group in Belize.

The Garinagu of southern Belize brought more than a dozen distinctive musical styles to the colony after their arrival in the early nineteenth century. They invented the most familiar Belizean folk music, known as *punta*. This style traces its roots to African rhythms and "call-and-response" singing of the original Garinagu settlers from the island of Saint Vincent. In this style of performance, a soloist sings out a phrase. A chorus of several people then repeats the phrase, sometimes with a musical variation. Several dances evolved from this singing, including

The late Andy Palacio, a leading punta performer, was the first musician in Belize to appear in foreign countries in a music video. He sang and played guitar in the video *Wátina*, which came out in 2007. The video was associated with Palacio's music album of the same name.

Brukdown musician Wilfred Peters sings and plays his accordion during a Creole festival in Belize City.

Andy Palacio was a well-known and influential musician in Belize. He blended traditional Belizean music with modern instruments and musical styles. He died in January 2008.

the circular *chumba*, still performed at weddings, holidays, and any well-attended social event.

Modern punta has adopted electric guitars and other contemporary instruments. Punta bands still feature traditional drums, made of mahogany and animal skins, as well as rattles made out of gourds filled with seeds. The leading artists of punta rock include Andy Palacio and Oral Fuentes, who leads the Oral Fuentes Reggae Band.

Younger Belizeans enjoy many international sounds, including reggae from Jamaica, highlife from Africa, and hip-hop from North America. Leroy Young, a Belizean rapper, has appeared on several albums and has written books of poetry. Allison Hemsley, another star rapper, rhymes onstage and on-screen under the name Dan Man.

To hear music by Belizean artists Andy Palacio, Wilfred Peters, Leroy Young, and others, go to the links at www.vgsbooks.com.

Food

The food of Belize includes tastes and cooking styles from Africa, the Caribbean, and Central America. Cooks prepare many of their dishes with blazing hot spices. They use sweet milk and sugar, to give the

Fried fish is served with a side of rice and beans. Rice and beans accompany almost every dish in Belize. Fresh fish is also widely available.

dishes a sweet and smooth texture. Fruit, especially mangoes, oranges, bananas, and limes, gives many Belizean dishes a unique flavor.

As Belize is a coastal nation, many kinds of seafood find their way onto restaurant menus and into home cooking. Lobster, shrimp, flounder, and barracuda are popular.

THE HOT STUFF

Every cook in Belize knows Marie Sharp's. This hot sauce comes in several different strengths, including Mild, Hot, Fiery, Belizean Heat, No Wimps Allowed, and Beware. Even Belizeans used to hot spicy food take the last variety with great care, adding only a few drops to their food.

Workers at the Marie Sharp's hot sauce factory fill bottles with the fiery liquid.

FRIED PLANTAINS

This recipe for ripe plantains is a favorite in Belize.

4 plantains

3 tablespoons vegetable oil or
  butter

1 tablespoon orange juice

1 tablespoon honey

1 cup sour cream

1. Select ripe plantains, with skins that are turning black but still have some yellow areas.
2. Peel the plantains, and slice them into thin rounds.
3. Heat oil or butter over high heat in a medium-sized frying pan. Carefully add plantain slices, and fry on one side for about five minutes, or until they are brown and soft. Use a spatula or tongs to turn the slices over, and cook for about five more minutes, or until the plantains are soft all the way through.
4. While the plantains are still hot, transfer them to a serving bowl. Add orange juice and stir gently. Finally, drizzle the honey over the plantains. Serve the fried plantains hot with a side of sour cream for dipping.

Serves 2 to 4

Rice and beans has long been the standard dinner meal. On the side, it accompanies dishes of stewed beef or fried chicken. Belizean rice and beans may include grated coconut as well as hot sauce and black pepper.

The plantain is a tropical fruit that resembles the banana, with a tougher texture. Belizeans prepare plantains fried in oil or butter and topped with sour cream, orange juice, or other preparations.

Spanish-speaking immigrants have added their own cuisine to the mix. Taco stands are a common sight on the streets of Belize City. Belizeans also enjoy *panades* (fried corn patties filled with fish or beans), as well as *garnaches* (tortillas topped with beans, vegetables, and cheese) and *salbutes* (hot, fried tacos).

Garinagu cuisine includes fish, plantains, coconut milk, vegetables, and herbs. *Hudut* is a simple dish of fish stewed in coconut milk. A boil-up is a heavy fish stew with several varieties of seafood, including conch, shrimp, and lobster.

Sports and Recreation

Belizeans enjoy individual as well as team sports. A few soccer and basketball clubs compete in semiprofessional leagues. Many towns

Mayan children in a rural village kick around a **soccer** ball.

have cricket pitches, where cricketers try their skill at a game imported from England. Cricket is a complex bat-and-ball game. Belize's organized amateur softball leagues compete successfully in international tournaments.

Golf and tennis are favored by those who can afford membership in a private club. Track-and-field athletes train for Olympic bids in the Marion Jones Sports Complex, named after the U.S. Olympic runner, whose mother was born in Belize. Belize first took part in the Summer Olympic Games in 1968 and since that time has sent male and female track athletes and cyclists to the Olympics.

Cycling has grown in popularity, with a Commonwealth Day race taking place every year between Belize City and San Ignacio. A canoe competition known as La Ruta Maya Belize River Challenge is a four-day contest that takes place in early March.

Many visitors come to Belize purely for the enjoyment of outdoor sports. Tourists enjoy hiking through the rain forest, rock climbing in the Maya Mountains, and mountain biking over rugged trails. Along the coast and in the islands, scuba diving and snorkeling are favorite activities. Those seeking to challenge the wind and weather try sailing, sea kayaking, and other sports.

▷ Religion

Belize is a mostly Roman Catholic nation, with an estimated 50 percent of modern Belizeans following this branch of Christianity. Roman Catholicism first arrived with the Spanish missionaries of the sixteenth and seventeenth centuries. It was not the only religion to find a place in Belize. British settlers were Anglicans. In addition, the Maya held to their traditional beliefs. In the Mayan view, natural deities oversee human events. A complex eighteen-month calendar sets out the proper days for important Mayan religious observations and rituals.

Worshippers in a Christian church in Dangriga incorporate traditional African instruments into the service.

As people from other Central American countries and Mexico arrived in the nineteenth century, Catholicism grew stronger. Catholic priests also came to teach. Most came from the United States. They built churches and schools, as well as Saint John's secondary school in Belize City. The Catholic Church still operates most of the schools in the country.

Other Belizeans belong to the Anglican Church of England. The country is home to Methodists, Presbyterians, and Mennonites as well. Other Protestant sects have come from the United States, including the Jehovah's Witnesses, the Mormons, and the Assemblies of God. In all, about 30 percent of all Belizeans are non-Catholic Christians. Another 10 percent or so follow other religions, such as Hinduism, Islam, or Buddhism. And the remaining 10 percent of people do not identify with any religion.

Many Belizeans combine the rituals and beliefs of more than one religion. The Garinagu, for example, have largely accepted Catholic Christianity. But they also continue to follow African practices honoring ancestors and appeasing natural spirits. The Maya, likewise, have combined Catholicism with traditional beliefs in gods of the rain, the sun, and the moon. Among the Creoles of Belize, a belief in magic and witchcraft has endured.

⊙ Holidays and Festivals

Public holidays in Belize include New Year's Day and Labor Day (May 1). Day of the Americas, in October, commemorates the arrival of Europeans in the Western Hemisphere. On the second Monday in

March, Belizeans celebrate Baron Bliss Day. This festival honors Baron Henry Edward Ernest Victor Bliss. In gratitude for the hospitality of Belizeans, Baron Bliss left his worldly goods to the country in 1926. May 24 is known as Commonwealth Day and celebrates the birthday of Queen Elizabeth II, who is the official head of state in Belize.

On September 10, Belizeans remember the Battle of Saint George's Caye, in which a ragtag group of British settlers held off a fleet of Spanish ships. Independence Day, celebrating the full sovereignty won in 1981, takes place on September 21. The Garinagu mark their arrival in Belize with Settlement Day, every November 19. River processions re-create the journey of the first Garinagu settlers.

Other holidays in Belize are religious in nature. Christmas and Easter are important Christian holidays that are the occasion for religious observances and family get-togethers. One very popular event is Carnival. This holiday falls right before Lent, a somber period leading up to Easter. In modern Belize, it is a festive occasion for parades, extravagant costumes, lively music, and traditional dance.

All Saints' Day and All Souls' Day are a pair of Christian holidays observed in Belize on November 1 and 2. All Saints' Day celebrates all Catholic saints, while All Souls' Day (also known as Los Finados, or Day of the Dead) honors the souls of those who have died. Celebrations include setting out food and drink for those departed souls and walking in candlelit processions to cemeteries. Both Mayan and mestizo populations in western Belize participate in this holiday.

Costumed dancers celebrating Independence Day march in a festive parade through a neighborhood of Belize City.

THE ECONOMY

During Belize's years as a colony, its economy was tied to the market for timber in Europe. For centuries, the British allowed loggers to exploit the colony's timber resources. Belize was sparsely populated, and there was little investment in industry or mining. The cities remained small and isolated. Few settlers moved into the countryside to farm the land.

In the twentieth century, heavy logging began to shrink Belize's forest regions. Belizean timber grew more difficult to harvest and ship. The colony began exporting sugarcane, as well as citrus fruits and seafood. Belize's economy still had to compete with other countries in Central America and the Caribbean. With little outside investment, it struggled to produce its goods at a cost that matched that of its neighbors. By the 1980s, the country was in dire straits financially. It lacked money for new development, and the government had a growing budget deficit, meaning that it spent more than it took in. A large loan from international banks helped Belize weather the crisis, but challenges remained.

After achieving independence in 1981, Belize began building new hotels, resorts, and roads. As a result, the tourist industry began to grow rapidly. Visitors arrived to explore Mayan ruins, coastal towns, and the offshore islands and diving sites. Tourist dollars brought new development to many areas. Resorts, hotels, and guided tours created new jobs. The economy recovered gradually through the 1990s.

Belize's gross domestic product, or GDP—the total value of all goods and services produced within the country—stands at more than $1 billion. The economy of Belize has been growing between 3 to 4 percent per year. This rate is one of the best in Central America or the Caribbean region. But Belize is vulnerable to rising energy prices, as it must import most of its oil. It also needs to invest in roads and public services. Finding better opportunities abroad, many Belizeans still leave the country after completing their education. Keeping skilled workers at home is key to the country's economic success.

Factories such as this one turn Belize's orange crop into juice concentrate for export.

Manufacturing and Mining

The small manufacturing sector in Belize serves the domestic market. Companies in Belize must compete with neighboring nations with a larger pool of labor and lower wages. This makes the costs of manufacturing higher in Belize and its products more expensive. Belize also lacks skilled engineers and technicians, many of whom emigrate for better opportunities abroad.

Manufacturing and mining make up about 14 percent of the GDP and employ approximately 8 percent of Belizean workers. The major industries process sugarcane and citrus products, manufacture clothing, and make fertilizers.

The small mining industry extracts basic construction materials, including sand, gravel, and clay. There are small limestone and marble quarries as well. A few adventurous people have attempted panning for gold and precious gemstones in Belizean rivers. They have found limited success, and the country has attracted no large commercial mining ventures.

Energy

During the 1980s, several foreign oil companies explored the waters off Belize for natural gas and crude oil. They found small deposits but not enough to make large-scale drilling worthwhile. Instead, Belize must import all of its fuel, and it generates much of its electricity through costly oil-fired generators. The rising cost of energy has affected many Belizean families and businesses. It also poses challenges for the tourist industry, as the costs of travel rise for visitors.

Belize's many fast-flowing streams hold the potential of a hydroelectric industry. But many of the rivers flow through remote areas and are hard to reach. A large investment would be required to build the needed water reservoirs.

Several companies are also exploring biofuels (fuels that come from recently living matter) and the use of recycled wood and waste products. These renewable energy resources might play a larger role in the future in driving vehicles and providing electricity.

◉ Foreign Trade

Belize has several important trading agreements with the United States and the European Union (an economic and political association of European nations). It also belongs to the Caribbean Community (CARICOM), an open market among the nations of the Caribbean region. By an agreement known as the U.S.-Caribbean Trade Partnership Act, signed in 2000, Belize can export many of its goods free of duty and taxes to the United States. This agreement has led to new U.S. investment in shrimp farming and the Belizean clothing industry.

The nation's major exports include clothing, seafood, bananas, and sugarcane. Sugarcane alone makes up about half of all exports.

Belize imports machinery, vehicles, consumer goods, food, and construction materials. The United States remains the most important source of imports and the largest buyer of exports. Belize also trades with Guatemala, Mexico, Canada, Japan, and Britain, as well as the nations of the Caribbean region.

Belize runs a trade deficit of about $300 million, with the country importing much more than it exports. A large part of its foreign exchange comes from Belizeans living and working abroad, who send money back home to relatives. These funds help sustain communities where industry and jobs are limited.

A worker places protective bags around bunches of bananas. The bags are coated with pesticides to protect the fruit from insects. Bananas are among Belize's chief agricultural export crops.

Transportation

Belize has a limited road network. Unpaved roads make up 1,433 miles (2,307 km), and paved roads total 351 miles (565 km). Four main highways serve the major towns and cities. Many of these highways have uncompleted sections, which slow traffic during the rainy season. There are no railways. The Stann Creek Railway is no longer used, as transporting goods by truck is less costly.

The famous Hummingbird Highway winds through the highlands of central and southern Belize, following part of the route of the old Stann Creek Railway. The paving of this road in the 1990s opened the region to rapid development. The Southern Highway runs to Punta Gorda.

Few Belizeans own cars. Instead, most use public buses to get around within cities and around the country. Water taxis ply the coastal waters between Belize City and the largest offshore islands. These fast craft also link Dangriga and other towns in the south with ports in Guatemala and Honduras.

Philip S. W. Goldson International Airport, outside Belize City, links Belize with North and South America and Europe. Until 2007 its runways were too short to accommodate the largest jet aircraft. In that year, the airport undertook major runway construction. Small airstrips serve the outlying towns and some of the islands.

Working harbors operate in Belize City, Big Creek, and Dangriga. These ports can handle only shallow-draft boats, however, such as fishing vessels and recreational boats. Small craft can navigate the Belize River, from the seacoast inland to the border with Guatemala.

Media and Communications

The print media in Belize carry on a lively debate on the country's politics, social issues, and business life. *Amandala* and the *Reporter* are the leading independent news weeklies. The PUP publishes its views on the issues in the weekly *Belize Times*. The UDP operates the *Guardian*. There are weekly papers in several small towns, and *Ambergris Today* appears on the largest island.

Most newspapers have a presence on the Internet. With the expense of telephones, many Belizeans have adopted the Internet as a more convenient means of private and business communication. When they do use the telephone, most Belizeans prefer to use mobile cell phones rather than landlines.

Belize has two national television stations. A local station operates in Orange Walk but has a limited broadcast range. Belizeans also enjoy satellite and cable broadcasts from Europe and North America. Listeners can tune into more than a dozen Belizean and foreign radio stations, with Love FM drawing the largest audience.

The Future

Although it is a small nation with relatively few resources, Belize has a promising future. The country is attracting foreign investment. Tourists are arriving at the rate of more than one million every year. The stable political climate has helped the nation progress and develop. Belize gained independence without war, and its opposing political parties hold regular elections peacefully.

The most important challenges facing Belize are social and environmental. An influx of permanent residents from Europe and North America is also having an effect. Belizeans are integrating new languages and cultures into their complex social mix. In addition, the country continues to struggle with issues such as violent crime, drug trafficking, human trafficking, and a black market. New construction is threatening the country's fragile ecosystems. Mangrove coasts and tropical forests are slowly disappearing, while new hotels and resorts crowd the offshore islands. The health of offshore corals and the barrier reef are also a major concern.

In addition, a large segment of the population still lives in poverty. In small towns and rural areas, Belizeans have limited options for schooling, health, and jobs. Because much of its food is imported, Belize also is vulnerable to rising prices. High energy costs drive up the price of many household goods including food. A surplus of fertile land, however, may help Belize to become more self-sufficient. As one of the most sparsely populated countries in the hemisphere, Belize also can accommodate newcomers. Immigration, of both people and businesses, may provide the key to a more prosperous future.

Construction workers build homes in Hopkins in the Stann Creek District.
Many new homes are built for foreigners choosing to move to Belize.

CA. 2500 B.C. The Maya build the city of Cuello, in northern Belize.

A.D. 250 The classic period of Mayan history begins, as Mayan civilization reaches the height of its development.

900 The Mayan civilization begins a slow decline that will continue for several centuries. Mayan cities will be abandoned, and the population will decline.

1502–1503 Christopher Columbus sails along the Caribbean coast of Central America but does not land there.

1511 A Spanish vessel shipwrecks off the coast of Belize. The Maya capture and imprison the crew, executing some members and enslaving others.

1544 The Spanish conquer the Mayan city of Tipu, the capital of the Mayan province of Dzuluinicob.

1638 Peter Wallace, a Scottish buccaneer, settles along the Belize River, the first European to settle in Belize. In the same year, the people of Tipu begin a rebellion against Spanish authority.

1670s More British settlers (Baymen) arrive in Belize, which is known at the time as the Bay Settlement. The settlers build small logging camps along the coast.

1798 Baymen and buccaneers defeat the Spanish at the Battle of Saint George's Caye.

1823 The Garinagu arrive in Honduras from the island of Saint Vincent. Soon afterward, some will move to Belize.

1833 The British government formally abolishes slavery in Belize and other British territories.

1847 The Caste War in Mexico's Yucatán begins. Over the following decades, this war drives thousands of Mexican refugees into northern Belize.

1854 Britain draws up a constitution for the government of its land claims in Central America, which will become British Honduras.

1862 Britain officially declares that British Honduras is a colony.

1865 The end of the Civil War in the United States brings refugees from the Confederacy to British Honduras.

1892 Belize Town becomes the capital of the colony of British Honduras.

1919 Black Belizean soldiers returning from World War I stage the Ex-Servicemen's Riot to protest racial discrimination in the colony.

1931 A powerful hurricane strikes the coast of Belize.

1954   The British government grants the right to vote to all
        adults who can read and write.

1961   Hurricane Hattie devastates Belize City. The government plans to
        move the capital to Belmopan.

1968   Athletes from Belize first participate in the Olympic Games (representing
        British Honduras) for the first time.

1970   Belmopan becomes the official capital of British Honduras.

1973   The name of British Honduras officially changes to Belize.

1981   Britain grants full independence to Belize. George Cadle Price becomes the first
        prime minister.

1982   Zee Edgell publishes her first novel, *Beka Lamb*. This book is the first novel published
        in a fully independent Belize.

1984   The United Democratic Party wins elections under the leadership of Manuel Esquivel.

1991   Guatemala recognizes independent Belize but continues to dispute the border between
        the two countries.

1998   The People's United Party and its new leader, Said Musa, win elections. Musa becomes
        prime minister.

2007   Garinagu musician Andy Palacio releases his final album. In October the Supreme Court
        of Belize recognizes the right of the Maya to keep mining, farming, and fishing rights
        on their ancestral lands.

2008   The UDP wins elections, and Dean Barrow becomes prime minister. Four athletes
        represent Belize at the Summer Olympics in Beijing, China.

COUNTRY NAME Belize

AREA 8,867 square miles (22,965 sq. km)

MAIN LANDFORMS Cayes and Barrier Reef, Coastal Lowlands, Central Plains, Western Highlands

HIGHEST POINT Doyle's Delight, 3,688 feet (1,124 m)

MAJOR RIVERS Belize, Bravo, Booth's, Hondo, Macal, Mopan, New

ANIMALS barracuda, jaguars, manatees, monkeys, ocelots, parrots, storks, tapirs, toucans, wild turkeys

CAPITAL CITY Belmopan

OTHER MAJOR CITIES Belize City, San Ignacio, Orange Walk, Dangriga

OFFICIAL LANGUAGE English

MONETARY UNIT Belize dollar. 100 cents = 1 dollar.

CURRENCY

The Belize dollar (BZ$) is the unit of currency in Belize. The government keeps the official exchange rate at two Belize dollars to one U.S. dollar, a currency that is also widely accepted in Belize. The BZ$ is divided into 100 cents. There are banknotes (paper money) of 2, 5, 10, 20, 50, and 100 dollars. Coins appear in values of 1, 5, 10, 25, and 50 cents, and 1 dollar. All Belizean banknotes carry a portrait of Queen Elizabeth II. Their reverse sides show important symbols of Belizean wildlife, such as the tapir and the toucan.

Currency Fast Facts

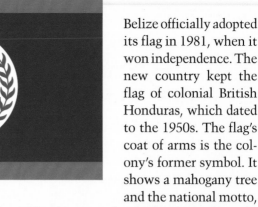

Belize officially adopted its flag in 1981, when it won independence. The new country kept the flag of colonial British Honduras, which dated to the 1950s. The flag's coat of arms is the colony's former symbol. It shows a mahogany tree and the national motto, *Sub Umbra Floreo*, which means "I prosper in the shade." On either side of the tree are two woodcutters, one holding an ax and one a paddle. The paddle symbolizes the river transport that brought mahogany logs to market. The central blue background represents the People's United Party, while the red horizontal stripes stand for the United Democratic Party.

Belize's national anthem is "Land of the Free," written by Samuel Alfred Haynes. The words are set to music by Selwyn Walford Young, a Belizean musician born in 1899. Haynes was a Belizean soldier who fought in World War I. He was also active in the movement for greater equality for black Belizeans and independence from Britain. The anthem was adopted in 1981, upon independence. The first verse and chorus of the anthem follow.

O, Land of the free by the Carib Sea,
Our manhood we pledge to thy liberty!
No tyrants here linger, despots must flee
This tranquil haven of democracy
The blood of our sires which hallows the sod,
Brought freedom from slavery oppression's rod,
By the might of truth and the grace of God,
No longer shall we be hewers of wood.

Chorus:
Arise! Ye sons of the Baymen's clan,
Put on your armors, clear the land!
Drive back the tyrants, let despots flee—
Land of the free by the Carib Sea!

For a link to a site where you can listen to Belize's national anthem, "Land of the Free," visit www.vgsbooks.com.

Flag **National Anthem**

PEN CAYETANO (b. 1954) A famous Garinagu musician, Pen Cayetano was born in Dangriga. He became a punta star after forming the Turtle Shell Band in 1979. He moved to Germany in 1990 and helped to start the Cayetanos. The band features several members of his large family.

ZELMA I. "ZEE" EDGELL (b. 1940) A writer born in Belize City, Zee Edgell has published four novels about life in Belize. She studied journalism in London, England, and at the University of the West Indies and for ten years worked as a reporter for a Belizean newspaper. Her books include *Beka Lamb*, which was the first novel published in independent Belize. Her novels *In Times Like These*, *The Festival of San Joaquin*, and *Time and the River* explore the history and complex society of Belize. Edgell has also taught creative writing at Kent State University in Ohio.

KALILAH ENRÍQUEZ (b. 1983) Enríquez is a poet and well-known radio host born in Belmopan. She hosts an FM morning show, *Wake Up Belize Morning Vibes*. She published her first book of poetry, *Unfettered*, in 2006.

TRICIA FLORES (b. 1979) Flores is a world-class long jumper. She has competed in many international events, including the 2008 Summer Olympics in Beijing, China. She also holds the Belize record for women's long jump, having once made a leap of more than 19.5 feet (5.94 m). Although no Belizean athletes won medals at the Beijing Olympics, Flores and her teammates were proud and excited to take part in the games.

ANGELA GEGG (b. 1979) Born in Belize City, Gegg is one of the nation's best-known artists and media personalities. Her traveling exhibitions of paintings and photography draw wide notice in Belize and throughout the Caribbean. She has written a book of essays and poetry, *The Light, the Dark, and Everything in Between*, and appears each year on Belize's Channel 7 as host of the annual televised Carnival celebrations.

PHILIP STANLEY WILBERFORCE GOLDSON (1923–2001) A newspaper editor who was born in Belize City, Goldson edited the *Belize Billboard*, which played an important role in the drive for independence. He also helped to found the People's United Party as well as the United Democratic Party, the two largest political parties in the country. Belize named its main international airport after him.

SAMUEL ALFRED HAYNES (1899–1971) Haynes was a Belizean soldier who fought for the British army in World War I. In 1919 Haynes—a black Belizean—led a demonstration against racial discrimination in British Honduras. Some historians think that this unrest helped spur on the independence movement as well. Haynes also wrote the poem "Land of the Gods," which became "Land of the Free," the Belizean national anthem.

EVAN X HYDE (b. 1947) Hyde is a writer and journalist born in Belize City. In 1969 he formed the United Black Association for Development (UBAD). The UBAD's goal was to fight for equal rights under the law for Belizeans of African descent. In addition, Hyde wrote several books on the history of black communities in Belize, including *Knocking Our Own Ting*, his first book. He also wrote *North Amerikkkan Blues* about his experiences as a student at Dartmouth College in New Hampshire. He edits *Amandala*, a leading weekly newspaper, and helped to establish KREM radio, a leading FM station.

EMORY KING (1931–2007) King was an author and historian of Belize who was born in Jacksonville, Florida. In 1955 King was shipwrecked in the Caribbean. Instead of returning to the United States, he settled in what was then British Honduras. He worked as a secretary for George Cadle Price, leader of the People's United Party, and became an editor of the *Belize Times*. King also appeared in several movies set in Belize.

PAUL NABOR (b. 1930) A musician born in Punta Gorda, Nabor performs in the *paranda* musical style, an older tradition of the Garinagu people. He plays guitar and sings, and in 1999, he was included on the album *Paranda*, produced by Andy Palacio. Nabor also leads a small Garinagu temple and is well known in his hometown as a healer and spirit medium (someone who communicates between people and the spirits of the dead).

BENJAMIN NICHOLAS (b. 1930) An artist and historian of the Garinagu people, Nicholas was born in Barranco, a village on the Belizean seacoast. He studied art in Guatemala and at the University of Minnesota. He returned to Belize but still exhibits his work in the United States, as well as in his home country. His paintings show the daily life of the Garinagu.

ANDY PALACIO (1960–2008) Palacio was a famous Garinagu musician born in Barranco. He lived for some time in Nicaragua, a Central American nation. After returning to Belize, he began writing songs in the Garifuna language as well as English. His records have sold in many foreign countries. They include *Til Da Mawning* and his last album, *Wátina*.

GEORGE CADLE PRICE (b. 1919) Born in Belize City, Price was a politician and leader of the independence movement in Belize. In 1950 Price helped to found the People's United Party, which he began leading in 1956 in the effort to win sovereignty for the colony of British Honduras. He served as mayor of Belize City from 1956 until 1962 and became Belize's first prime minister in 1981, the year of independence. He served a second term from 1989 until 1993.

Sights to See

ACTUN TUNICHIL MUKNAL This site is a series of limestone caves. These caves shelter Mayan artifacts such as pottery, as well as burial chambers containing Mayan skeletons hundreds of years old.

AMBERGRIS CAYE This is the largest offshore island in Belizean waters, and its setting presents stunning seacoast views. Fishing, exploring San Pedro (the island's main settlement), and diving offshore are all popular activities. In addition, Bacalar Chico National Park lies at the northern end of the island. This park highlights mangrove forests, manatees, and other native flora and fauna.

CARACOL The largest Mayan site in Belize, Caracol was the center of a prosperous farming area. Archaeologists have been digging at the site for decades and have yet to uncover the entire city. But visitors can already see many impressive and historic ruins here.

COCKSCOMB BASIN WILDLIFE SANCTUARY AND JAGUAR PRESERVE This forest preserve in southern Belize is the only one in the world created to protect the jaguar. The preserve includes several miles of walking trails and Victoria Peak, the second-highest mountain in Belize, at 3,681 feet (1,122 m).

HALF MOON CAYE NATURAL MONUMENT This nature preserve is dedicated to the protection of the rare red-footed booby, a slow-moving bird with white feathers and a long, gray beak. The bird was nearly hunted to extinction.

HUMMINGBIRD HIGHWAY This scenic road in central Belize follows part of the route of the historic Stann Creek Railway. Hummingbird Highway winds through dense forest and past large citrus orchards and plantations. The road, between Belmopan and Dangriga, is about 56 miles (90 km).

IX CHEL FARM At this facility in western Belize, scientists are studying the medicinal properties of various tropical plants. The farm includes a self-guided Rainforest Medicine Trail, where visitors learn how the Maya used plants to cure disease and heal injuries.

LAMANAI Located on the shores of the New River Lagoon, Lamanai is a ceremonial Mayan city. Lamanai is one of the largest Mayan sites in Belize and includes three restored temples. The site was inhabited for more than three thousand years, until the seventeenth century.

SHARK RAY ALLEY This well-known snorkeling and scuba-diving site lies off the southern shores of Ambergris Caye. Nurse sharks and stingrays circle divers in 8 feet (2.4 m) of clear water. The fish are harmless—if you don't disturb them.

Baymen: British settlers in Belize, who built small logging camps and opposed Spanish attempts to seize the territory through the late eighteenth century

Bay Settlement: the former name for the territory settled by British sailors and log cutters in what is modern Belize

boil-up: a fish stew made with several varieties of seafood, especially popular among Creole and Garinagu cooks

British Honduras: the colony founded by Great Britain in the nineteenth century, later changed to Belize

Caste War: a conflict that began in 1847 in the Yucatán, a southern province of Mexico. This war, which lasted until 1901, drove many refugees into northern Belize.

cayes: the thousands of small islands lying off the coast of Belize, many of which are uninhabited

chicle: a gum harvested from the sapodilla tree. British Honduras exported chicle throughout the middle of the twentieth century to chewing gum manufacturers.

colony: a territory ruled and occupied by a foreign power

Creole: an ethnic group of people who have mixed European and African ancestry and who speak a distinct language known as Kriol

Garinagu: also known as Garifuna, people descended from African slaves and native peoples, who migrated to Central America from the island of Saint Vincent in the early nineteenth century

gross domestic product (GDP): a measure of the total value of goods and services produced within a country's boundaries in a certain amount of time (usually one year), regardless of the citizenship of the producers

literacy: the ability to read and write a basic sentence. A country's literacy rate is one indicator of its level of human development.

logwood: a wood used to make dye. Logwood was the most important export of the first British settlers in Belize.

Mennonites: a group of religious families who began settling near the Hondo River in northern Belize in 1959.

mestizo: a person of mixed European (usually Spanish) and indigenous ancestry

missionary: a religious worker who works in a foreign country. Missionaries often attempt to convert people to Christianity, but they may also build hospitals, establish schools, and do other community work.

People's United Party (PUP): name of the leading political party in Belize, which led the country at the time of its full independence in 1981

United Democratic Party (UDP): a Belizean political party that first won elections in 1984 under the leadership of Manuel Esquivel

Ball, Joseph W. *Cahal Pech, the Ancient Maya, and Modern Belize: The Story of an Archaeological Park*. San Diego: San Diego State University Press, 1993.
This book describes the ancient site of Cahal Pech, in the Cayo District, and how the government of Belize transformed the site into a modern tourist attraction.

Barry, Tom. *Inside Belize*. Albuquerque, NM: Resource Center Press, 1995.
The author presents detailed information on the society, economy, culture, history, and politics of modern Belize.

Grant, C. H. *The Making of Modern Belize*. Cambridge: Cambridge University Press, 1976.
A scholarly book on the political scene in Belize as it struggled for freedom from colonial rule, this title deals with social divisions within the country and how they affected the independence movement.

Europa World Year Book, 2008. Vol. 1. London: Europa Publications, 2008.
Covering Belize's recent history, economy, and government, this annual publication also provides a wealth of statistics on population, employment, trade, and more.

McKillop, Heather Irene. *The Ancient Maya: New Perspectives*. New York: W. W. Norton, 2006.
The author reviews the possible answers to the many puzzles surrounding the Maya: their system of writing, their way of daily life, and the reasons for the collapse of Mayan civilization.

———. *Salt: White Gold of the Ancient Maya*. Gainesville: University Press of Florida, 2002.
This book describes a salt-making factory built by the Maya on the coast of Belize and speculates on the system of salt making and trading in the Mayan world.

Miller, Carlos Ledson. *Belize: A Novel*. Philadelphia: Xlibris, 2000.
This novel traces the strivings of a logging family through several decades of modern Belizean history.

New York Times Company. *The* New York Times *on the Web*. 2008.
http://www.nytimes.com (October 22, 2008).
This online version of the newspaper offers current news stories along with an archive of articles on Belize.

PRB. "PRB 2008 World Population Data Sheet." *Population Reference Bureau*. 2008.
http://www.prb.org (October 22, 2008).
This annual statistics sheet provides a wealth of data on Belize's population, birthrate and death rate, fertility rate, infant mortality rate, and other useful demographic information.

Selected Bibliography

Rabinowitz, Alan. *Jaguar: One Man's Struggle to Establish the World's First Jaguar Preserve.* **New York: Arbor House, 1986.**
A zoologist describes his study of the jaguars of the Belizean forest and how he convinced the government of Belize to establish the Cockscomb Basin Wildlife Sancuary and Jaguar Preserve, the world's only jaguar preserve.

Setzekorn, William David. *Formerly British Honduras: A Profile of the New Nation of Belize.* **Athens: Ohio University Press, 1981.**
This title is an overview of Belizean geography, culture, and history from the ancient Maya through the colonial period.

Simmons, Donald C. *Confederate Settlements in British Honduras.* **Jefferson, NC: McFarland, 2001.**
This book tells the story of Civil War Southerners, soldiers as well as civilians, who fled to British Honduras during and after the war, settling in Belize City and several other towns.

Thompson, P. A. B. *Belize: A Concise History.* **Oxford, UK: Macmillan Caribbean, 2005.**
The author gives a useful and brief outline of Belize history, from the ancient Mayan civilization to the era of independence in the twentieth century.

Twigg, Alan. *Understanding Belize: A Historical Guide.* **Madeira Park, BC: Harbour Publishing, 2006.**
This book gives detailed historical and cultural information on Belize, tracing the origins of several of the country's modern conflicts and problems, both natural and social.

Wright, Ronald. *Time among the Maya: Travels in Belize, Guatemala, and Mexico.* **New York: Grove Press, 2000.**
The author describes how the Maya have managed to adapt themselves to colonialism and the modern world. The book includes interesting and thorough information on the Mayan calendar and system of timekeeping.

Further Reading and Websites

Ambergriscaye.com
http://www.ambergriscaye.com
This website provides information about the largest island in Belize, with pages on wildlife, diving sites, history, and local culture and food.

Behnke, Alison. *Cooking the Central American Way*. Minneapolis: Lerner Publications Company, 2005.
This cookbook presents a selection of recipes from Belize and the surrounding region. Cooks throughout Central America use many of the same ingredients and methods to prepare meals.

Belizean Journeys
http://www.belizeanjourneys.com
This guide to Belizean culture and natural environment includes articles, photo galleries, and multimedia presentations.

Belize: A Virtual Guide
http://www.belizeexplorer.com
This site features a gallery of photos and information about the natural and man-made sights of interest in Belize.

Belize by Natural Light
http://www.belizenet.com/
This photo essay of Belize is combined with useful information for travelers, business visitors, and people who want to move to the country.

Belize News
http://www.belizenews.com
The website of the national newspaper of Belize, this site provides news, weather, maps, visitor information, and a "Photo of the Day" feature.

Coe, Michael D. *The Maya*. New York: Thames and Hudson, 2005.
This popular guide is an important source for the history and archaeology of the Maya, used by students as an introduction and by experts as a reliable reference book.

Day, Nancy. *Your Travel Guide to the Ancient Mayan Civilization*. Minneapolis: Twenty-First Century Books, 2001.
This title prepares readers for a trip back to the time of the Maya, including which cities to visit, how to get around, what to wear, and how to fit in with the locals.

Duran, Victor Manuel, ed. *An Anthology of Belizean Literature*. Lanham, MD: University Press of America, 2007.
This collection presents Belizean stories written in four different languages: English, Spanish, Creole, and Garifuna.

Edgell, Zee. *Beka Lamb*. Portsmouth, NH: Heinemann, 1992.
This novel tells the story of a twelve-year-old girl who experiences life's many ups and downs while her country wins its independence. This was the first novel published in independent Belize.

Kops, Deborah. *Palenque.* **Minneapolis: Twenty-First Century Books, 2008.**

This book tells about the rediscovery and subsequent unearthing of the ancient Maya city of Palenque. The book describes in detail how archaeologists uncovered the ancient ruins and how they pieced together their findings to better understand how the ancient civilization may have lived.

Tedlock, Dennis. *Popul Voh: The Definitive Edition of the Mayan Book of the Dawn of Life and the Glories of Gods and Kings.* **New York: Touchstone, 1996.**

This is an ancient Mayan book that describes the creation of the world. The book is illustrated with Mayan hieroglyphs, many of which have only recently been deciphered.

vgsbooks.com
http://www.vgsbooks.com

Visit vgsbooks.com, the home page of the Visual Geography Series®. You can get linked to all sorts of useful online information, including geographical, historical, demographic, cultural, and economic websites. The vgsbooks.com site is a great resource for late-breaking news and statistics.

Captions for photos appearing on cover and chapter openers:

Cover: A wooden pier juts into a lake in Placencia, Belize.

pp. 4–5 Palm trees ring the sandy shores of a small fishing village on the coast of Belize.

pp. 8–9 Belize's barrier reef, made of coral, is one of the country's great natural treasures.

pp. 20–21 Ancient Mayan handprints cover the walls of Actun Uayazba Kab, or Handprint Cave, in west central Belize.

pp. 38–39 Belizean schoolgirls in their marching band uniforms celebrate Settlement Day.

pp. 46–47 A Creole man from Gales Point, near Dangriga, smiles from the window of his houseboat. Belizeans speak several languages, including Kriol.

pp. 58–59 A long row of trucks loaded with sugarcane heads for the processing plant before export. Sugar accounts for nearly half of Belize's exports.

Photo Acknowledgments
The images in this book are used with the permission of: © SuperStock, Inc./ SuperStock, pp. 4–5; © XNR Productions, pp. 6, 10; © Norbert Wu/Science Faction/Getty Images, pp. 8–9; © Panoramic Images/Getty Images, p. 11; © Gerry Lemmo, pp. 13, 15, 16 (right); AP Photo/Brennan Linsley, p. 14; © Cory Langley, pp. 16 (left), 40 (top); © Peter Essick/Aurora/Getty Images, p. 17; © DEA/ M. BORCHI/De Agostini Picture Library/Getty Images, p. 18; © Stephen Alvarez/ National Geographic/Getty Images, pp. 20–21; © age fotostock/SuperStock, pp. 23, 58–59; Private Collection/Peter Newark Pictures/The Bridgeman Art Library, p. 25; The Art Archive, p. 27; © Bill Hormann, http://www.mitchell -hedges.com, p. 30; AP Photo, p. 31; AP Photo/Jack Rutledge, p. 33; © Bettmann/ CORBIS, p. 34; © Juan Manuel Herrera, Organization of American States, p. 36; © Danita Delimont/Alamy, pp. 38–39, 40 (bottom), 56; © Michael J. Balick/Peter Arnold, Inc., p. 42; © Jim West/Alamy, pp. 43, 53 (bottom), 62, 65; © John Sones/ Lonely Planet Images, p. 44; © James Strachan/Stone/Getty Images, pp. 46–47; © Martin Spragg/Art Directors & TRIP, p. 48; © david sanger photography/Alamy, p. 49; *Beluria Rug* by Delvin "Pen" Cayetano © 2009 Artists Rights Society (ARS), New York / VG Bild-Kunst, Bonn, p. 50; © Tony Rath Photography, p. 51; © Sarah Lee/eyevine/ZUMA Press, p. 52; © Anthony Plummer/Lonely Planet Images/ ZUMA Press, p. 53 (top); © Index Stock Imagery/Photolibrary, p. 55; AP Photo/ John Moore, p. 57; © Kenneth Garrett/National Geographic/Getty Images, p. 60; © Nicolas Russell/The Image Bank/Getty Images, p. 61; © iStockphoto.com/ Francisco Orellana, p. 63; © iStockphoto.com/Nell Redmond, p. 68; © Laura Westlund/Independent Picture Service, p. 69.

Front Cover: © DEA/M. BORCHI/De Agostini Picture Library/Getty Images. Back Cover: NASA.